THE JESUS LIBRARY
edited by Michael Green

The Hard Sayings of Jesus
F. F. Bruce

Jesus: Lord & Savior
F. F. Bruce

The Teaching of Jesus
Norman Anderson

The Evidence for Jesus
R. T. France

The Supremacy of Jesus
Stephen Neill

The Healings of Jesus
Michael Harper

The Empty Cross of Jesus
Michael Green

Jesus, Man of Prayer
Margaret Magdalen

The Counselling of Jesus
Duncan Buchanan

Jesus and Power
David Prior

The Example of Jesus
Michael Griffiths

THE JESUS LIBRARY
Michael Green, series editor

The Counselling of Jesus

Duncan Buchanan

INTERVARSITY PRESS
DOWNERS GROVE, ILLINOIS 60515

© 1985 by Duncan Buchanan

Published in the United States of America by InterVarsity Press, Downers Grove, Illinois, with permission from Hodder and Stoughton Limited, England.

InterVarsity Press is the book-publishing division of Inter-Varsity Christian Fellowship, a student movement active on campus at hundreds of universities, colleges and schools of nursing. For information about local and regional activities, write IVCF, 233 Langdon St., Madison, WI 53703.

Cover illustration: Janice Skivington

ISBN 0-87784-931-5
ISBN 0-87784-933-1 (The Jesus Library set)

Printed in the United States of America

Library of Congress Cataloging in Publication Data

Buchanan, Duncan, 1935-
   The counselling of Jesus.

   (The Jesus library)
   Bibliography: p.
   1. Jesus Christ—Counseling methods.   2. Pastoral
counseling—Biblical teaching.   3. Bible. N.T.
Gospels—criticism, interpretation, etc.   I. Title.
II. Series.
BT590.C78B83   1985   253.5   85-19736
ISBN 0-87784-931-5

---

17   16   15   14   13   12   11   10   9   8   7   6   5   4   3   2
97   96   95   94   93   92   91   90   89   88

Editor's Preface

The evangelists tell us of Jesus that 'he knew what was in man.' If that is so, then it is of vital importance in an age when so many people are cracking up, to turn to Jesus Christ and examine afresh the ways in which he approached people in need, laid bare the source of their trouble, and offered his aid. Alas, it is all too rare to find a book which leads us into the counselling of Jesus. It is acknowledged on all sides that he is the greatest psychiatrist of all time, and yet even Christians tend to look everywhere else for insight into counselling, than to Jesus himself. Counselling is a major industry in many industrial societies in the world, not least in the U.S.A., yet how few of the insights and methods used owe anything to Jesus Christ? It is one of the many ways in which the church has surrendered to the spirit of the age that, when she does at length get round to counselling, she sits at the feet of mentors other than her Master.

It is not so with the Warden of St. Paul's Theological College, Grahamstown. He is one of the senior Christian leaders in South Africa, universally respected for the way he has led the College for many years, and made it one of the most spiritually vital (not to mention interracial) theological seminaries anywhere in the world. The Church in South Africa has been greatly helped and enlivened by the charismatic movement, and Canon Buchanan is richly gifted by the Holy Spirit and makes use of these gifts in counselling. But he is also a man who loves people, has a warm heart and a shrewd head, and has read widely on the subject. He is so much a 'people's person' that he has not written a book before this. Instead he has left his mark on countless lives, for he is greatly sought out as a counsellor and a spiritual director. I count myself particularly fortunate to have persuaded him to contribute this book to the Jesus Library. He and Di were the most marvellous hosts to Rosemary and myself during two months sabbatical in January and February, 1984, and not only were we treated with much love and laughter, not only were we helped personally at depth by our dear hosts, but we had the opportunity of seeing them in action over a considerable period. I was convinced, before leaving St. Paul's, that Duncan would write an outstanding book, showing us the counselling approach of Jesus, and enabling us to enter into it. I have not been disappointed. And neither will you be. This book deserves wide circulation among all who seek to help other people with psychological and emotional hurts in the name of Jesus. I know of nothing quite like it.

Michael Green

Preface

A book of this sort is inevitably the product of many encounters throughout one's life. The influence of my parents and the particular ability of my late mother to communicate love to others has been an influence which I need to acknowledge.

Over the years, teaching counselling at St Paul's College, Grahamstown, has refined this book, as the ideas, insights and skills have been brought to light and battered into submission.

Michael Green and his delightful wife Rosemary spent six weeks with us and it was during that time that the basic outline of this book was committed to paper, and the ideas discussed in detail. I am grateful to Michael for asking me to try to focus my thoughts and experiences for this book. John Freeth, Rector of St John's Parish, Wynberg, should have written this book, and would doubtless have done it better. I am grateful to him for his gracious support and ideas which have been extraordinarily helpful. The Reverend "Neb" Neser has read parts of the book and made some really valuable criticisms resulting in important changes.

I must place on record my thanks to the Council of St Paul's College for giving me the extra leave I needed to do the basic writing and to my colleagues on the staff of St Paul's who so enthusiastically encouraged me. Elizabeth and George Hunter made their delightful cottage on the Southern Cape coast available to us. Their son Andrew, a student at St Paul's, suggested we went there, and pushed us in that direction with great conviction! The Reverend Chris Ahrends, a former student at St Paul's, allowed us to invade the privacy of his home and gave us the quiet and hospitality necessary to see this book to its final stages. Chris was also responsible for suggesting the important distinction between empathy and compassion. Mrs Margie Hare very lovingly volunteered to translate my handwriting into typescript and Mrs Daphne Manley has been responsible for the final draft – a terrifying task after I had mutilated Margie's beautifully typed first draft.

Throughout this whole enterprise my wife Di and our two daughters Anne and Jean have given me enormous support and encouragement. Di in particular was prepared to sit late into the night at that seaside cottage while I wrote and was calm, loving and enthusiastic for the project. She has since then read the book and made many suggestions which have helped straighten out my convoluted English and clarify what I have been trying to communicate. It is a matter of joy to me that this book will be completed a few weeks before our twenty-fifth wedding anniversary. It is my gift to her, with gratitude and love.

Introduction

It would be a legitimate question to ask "Why yet another book on counselling?" The first, and perhaps obvious answer is that, as far as I know, no book has been written which pays attention specifically to the way Jesus counselled. But that would only be part of the reason for attempting this book.

I have always been fascinated by people. As a boy, I would watch people, any people, for hours, to the despair of my parents. I enjoyed people too. I still find the prospect of meeting new people an exciting and rewarding experience. There is so much to learn, so much to give, every person one meets adds to oneself a little more of what it means to be human.

Ever since I can remember, I had the example of parents who believed in God and practised that belief. One of my most profound childhood memories is seeing my father kneeling nightly at his bed locked in prayer. So it was natural to see people in relation to God, and to expect to see and experience God in people. I still do, which is why meeting people is so exciting.

People, as I soon discovered in myself and others, are sinful – wilful, irrational and selfish. They make a mess of their lives with consummate ease – and try as they may, they are not good at putting things together again. Money, effort, energy – all the king's horses and all the king's men – cannot add up to new life or personal problems solved. So counselling has a primary place in Christian ministry. There are the great souls who, under God, are responsible for changing nations and destinies. Most of us are called upon to help in

God's process of changing individuals and communities. God's work involves many aspects – healing, relationships, attitudes, repentance, new life, death to pride and self. It involves breaking down hardness of heart, fear, indifference, and always at some point there are people searching for peace, security, love and freedom.

As I have become involved in the Christian ministry, I have been drawn into the process of counselling, of the one-to-one involvement with people whose lives are incomplete and who do not know how they can grow. For nearly twenty years I have had the privilege of being on the staff of St Paul's College in Grahamstown and have had the task of trying to teach counselling. Fortunately, I have always been involved in the process as well, so it has never been an entirely theoretical course. For several years I was the Anglican Chaplain to a local mental hospital and found the relationships with staff and patients stimulating and very rewarding, as were the new insights gained into the intricate mechanisms of the human mind and emotions. I had done courses in counselling while training for the Ministry, but over the years, the presuppositions with which I had worked seemed to me to never quite fit the bill. I had been brought up on the Rogerian approach and have been influenced by Hiltner,[1] Clinebell[2] and Wise.[3] I have found myself agreeing with Rollo May[4] – for a while. A breakthrough came, however, when I had the privilege of going on a course run by Frank Lake.[5] He at least started where I believed all counselling *must* start – with Jesus. His dynamic life cycle was – and still is – for me a key to a truly biblical understanding of man. More important, I found Lake a man of deep prayer and delightful humour and humanity. It was as if all that I wanted to teach was focused in his teaching and personality.

I still find him stimulating and it will be evident how much I owe him in the pages which lie ahead. But somehow even that has not been enough – for even he did not go where I believed the Christian counsellor ought to go.

For several years in my own teaching, I have tried to

develop an attitude to counselling, more than seeking to impart skills or techniques. We can help people to look for certain things in an interview, but unless that person can take with him something more than skill, he will not be much use.

My greatest reaction, however, has been against the idea that counselling is somehow an activity which is divided into "schools". I find, for example, the lampooning of non-directive counselling by Jay Adams[6] as offensive as the disdainful rejection of any form of directive counselling by those in other camps. Neither do I believe that counselling can be reduced to clear-cut and neat steps – desirable though that may be.

As I have counselled, I have found myself using just about every technique I have come across, from directive and nouthetic to non-directive,[7] to the insights of Ruth Carter Stapleton,[8] to the rather amazing insights of Kenneth McAll,[9] to the newest theories suggested by Frank Lake[10] in his most recently published book, shortly before he died. I have found the insights of Roger Hurding[11] extraordinarily helpful, and his illustrations quite brilliant in their simplicity while getting at the heart of the issues described. All of them are valuable, because as I look at Jesus, I see him using them too. He is not tied to one style of counselling – only to an absolute commitment to bringing people into the wholeness of the Kingdom of God. So this book tries to look at the presuppositions which Jesus used and to see what we can learn from him in the counselling process.

There is yet another reason why I believe a book such as this needs to be written. Over the years, the world of psychology and its related disciplines, especially social work, have almost "cornered the market" on counselling. Many people believe that counselling is virtually the sole prerogative of those disciplines. I do not agree. I have learnt a tremendous amount from them, and I do not want to suggest that they have nothing to offer. I have come across too many sensitive, incredibly perceptive and able counsellors in those fields to feel anything other than admiration and respect for them. The

literature too is enormously useful. But I do believe that the
Christian has within his own traditions of prayer, Scripture,
worship and ethic and most particularly the Gospels themselves, such a treasury of resources for the development of
really creative relationships, that he has no need to be
ashamed or fearful of what he has to offer. The relationships
which Jesus developed and which are reported in the Gospels
are themselves unbelievably fruitful for helping us to understand the nature of new life in him, and how this is communicated in our own relationships and in times of stress.

It does not follow that this in any way purports to be a
textbook on counselling. That is not its aim. Rather its
purpose is to try to help people to an awareness of Jesus as
counsellor and to learn from him. In the process I will not be
following any "line" or "School of Counselling".

In trying to look at Jesus as he is depicted and reported in
the Gospels, I am very conscious that I am entering a
minefield of disagreement amongst the scholars. I do not want
to ignore that scholarship for in many ways I am dependent
upon it. Yet we do see Jesus in the Gospels, and the way the
Gospel writers present the incidents and exchanges of our
Lord's life teaches us an enormous amount about the counselling ministry. It is not easy to isolate the counselling of
Jesus from the rest of his ministry; so as we look at the
incidents in the Gospels we will concentrate on the whole
relationship with those around him, and not simply his
words.

Alan Paton once made a remark in my hearing which I
believe is essential to the Christian ministry. He said, "It is the
missionary's responsibility to keep the convert's eyes on
Jesus, so that he does not see the Christians." My prayer is
that in counselling we may help many to keep their eyes on
Jesus – and so find abundant life.

Chapter
1

"Jesus was the best psychiatrist who has ever lived." Those words were spoken by a medical doctor, who lectured on the subject of general practice at a medical school. We were at a conference on counselling and had been moved by the presentation of Frank Lake as he helped us, medical men and clergy, through the intricacies of people and their problems, and to insights which he shared with us about Jesus. This particular doctor had, as I remember, gone home and read most of one of the Gospels the previous night, and had then made his statement.

I remember asking him why and his answer was something like this: "He understands people, treats them as individuals, will not allow them to make excuses for themselves, and gives them a completeness which no one else has been able to give." That judgment is correct. Jesus *is* unique in his whole ministry; in his relationships with people he is unsurpassed. Within the categories in which the doctor thought, Jesus *was* the best of all psychiatrists. Depending on their categories of thought others could describe him as the most loving of all people; or the most complete; or the most discerning. Jesus is the universal man, and it is very difficult to isolate any one aspect of his personality or ministry. They all interrelate to make a person of whom at the best we can catch only a very satisfying though tantalising glimpse.

Over the years the evaluation of that doctor has stayed with me and I have found myself puzzling as to how Jesus reached that completeness of personality and perfection of ministry. Clearly he has a wholeness and an inner strength which derives from his relation with the Father, and equally from his very nature: sinless and overwhelmingly loving.

Facing the sinful world, Jesus's task of salvation involves total opposition to the forces which enslave and destroy mankind. So, if we are to gain insight from his relationship with the Father, and how that helped him come to terms with the emotions and fears of his manhood at odds with the powers which sought to enslave him, we must be aware of those forces, set as they are against the backdrop of a cosmic struggle for the very soul of mankind, and of the basis of his relationship with the Father.

The Kingdom of God vs the kingdom of Satan

Jesus comes into a world already prepared in some form by John the Baptist. He comes preaching repentance and the coming of the Kingdom of God.[1] It is a declaration that a new initiative by God will usher in a new dispensation; that the power of God is unleashed upon the forces of Satan, to break those forces and give men the opportunity of life lived in relation to God. It requires a positive and definite response from those who hear; the kingdom cannot be taken for granted, nor can it be assumed that birth into Judaism gives a right, which does not require repentance.

Essential to Jesus's mission is his awareness and, indeed, his use of the authority (*exousia*) of God. Again and again the crowds are reported as being amazed because of his power or authority.[2] Jesus's ministry is focused on one thing only – to bring people into the kingdom of God, so that living under the authority of God, people may once more be brought into that relationship with God which was broken at the Fall.

The Gospels are unanimous that the forces of evil or the kingdom of Satan, or (in John) the forces of darkness, are seeking to overcome and indeed overwhelm the world and reign supreme. Men and women, individually, are caught in the reign of evil; so are nations and societies. Jesus comes to bring people into the Kingdom of God, and for that to happen he has clearly to understand his own mission, and the power of the forces against which he is pitted; he *has* to be an authority on sin, and recognise it when he meets it; he has to be aware of the forces which seek to overpower him or deflect his purpose. All these are dependent upon his relationship with the Father.

Abba

J. Jeremias insists that "Abba" as an address to God in the prayers of Jesus expresses the *heart of Jesus's relationship to God*. "He spoke to God as a child to its father: confidently and securely, and yet at the same time reverently and obediently."[3]

Abba is not, as some might want, the address of an infant, it is not "Daddy", as I used to think, but it expresses an intimacy which is unknown in the Old Testament and an awareness of a relationship which cannot be broken. Jeremias insists that underlying every instance of "Father" or "the Father" in the Gospels is the use of the word Abba.[4]

It is a remarkable word, for it underscores the intimacy of a new relationship, and also emphasises Jesus's *exousia*. At the heart of Jesus's mission to attack and destroy the forces of evil, lies the sure knowledge of the Father as "Abba", that as he extends his mission outwards, his fundamental relationship with the Father cannot break. We shall see that throughout his ministry, Jesus comes back to Abba, both in prayer, and it seems within himself, and from the treasures of that relationship, faces sin and evil. This relationship is explicitly worked out in two specific instances – the baptism of Jesus and the remarkable saying recorded in Matthew 11:25–30.

The baptism of Jesus

In all three synoptic accounts of the baptism of Jesus, there is an insistence on the descent of the Spirit and the voice which declares, "Thou art my beloved Son; with thee I am well pleased." (In Matthew, the voice seems to be reassuring the Baptist, but the effect of designating Jesus as Son is the same.) It is not, of course, that Jesus became the Messiah at this point. Mark's use of the word *arche* (beginning) in his opening words, suggests that, at creation, as well as with the advent of Jesus on earth, Jesus was Messiah. The Gospel has a cosmic reality which cannot be pinned to one incident, no matter how important, in the life of Jesus. Jesus is Messiah and that is part of God's plan for creation. What is significant here is that he receives confirmation as to his status as he is about to begin his public ministry, and also is overwhelmed by his relationship with the Father.

In the Old Testament and indeed in the New, the son, especially the firstborn, is in effect already the inheritor of the father's property; he has the right to it, as well as the authority which comes with it. That is at least part of the impact of the parable of the prodigal son. The elder son had an even greater inheritance and a greater authority. That relationship was a formal and a legal one. For Jesus to be called Son meant that he had the authority of the Father, an authority which was quickly recognised by demon and crowd alike, and he had a relationship which so rooted him in the Father that he was able to call the Father Abba. So at the heart of his ministry is this deep relationship; one so strong that it can withstand the pressures and onslaughts of sin and Satan, and sustain him to the end.[5]

Matthew 11:25–30:   I thank thee, Father

"I thank thee, Father, Lord of heaven and earth, that thou hast hidden these things from the wise and understanding and revealed them to babes; yea Father for such was thy gracious will. All things have been delivered to me by my Father; and no one knows the Son except the Father, and no one knows the Father except the Son and anyone to whom the Son chooses to reveal him. Come to me, all who labour and are heavy laden, and I will give you rest. Take my yoke upon you and learn from me; for I am gentle and lowly in heart, and you will find rest for your souls. For my yoke is easy, and my burden is light."

Some have thought that this passage ought to be in John's Gospel and that somehow it has crept into Matthew's! What is remarkable is the absolute assurance that Jesus's sonship is the focal point for all revelation. Jeremias believes that v. 27 must be understood: "*Just as* only a father (really) knows his son, so only a son (really) knows his father."[6] The final line, "and anyone to whom the Son chooses to reveal him" is therefore a logical conclusion. Jeremias sums up his argument thus: "Matthew 11:27 is a central statement about the mission of Jesus. His Father has granted Him the revelation of Himself as completely as only a father can disclose himself to his son. Therefore, only Jesus can pass on to others the real knowledge of God."[7]

So again we have a declaration of a relationship which lies at the heart of Jesus's ministry and sustains him as he reveals the Father. It is not surprising that, strong in the Abba relationship, he is able to be so unequivocal in v. 28: "Come to me all who labour and are heavy laden and I will give you rest." Sure in the knowledge of God the Father and aware of his Father's presence, he can afford to let the weak and weary lean on him, and indeed calls them to do so. But the concept of Sonship and the ultimate relationship with the Father has other consequences as well.

Servant
It is not necessary for me to go into the implications of servanthood which lie at the root of the words of the Father at Jesus's baptism. It is well known that Isaiah 42:1 is here quoted and obedience is quite clearly an essential quality of servanthood. The servant in Isaiah is to be obedient even when all the evidence points to the horrifying possibility that God has abandoned him. He is rejected not because of his disobedience or sinful rebelliousness, but precisely because

he *is* obedient. He leans continually on his absolute belief that God has called him and will not abandon him.[8]

The servant is ultimately vindicated because he is obedient in circumstances where public opinion demands what for him would be disobedience. Jesus's sonship, indeed his ministry, is integrally tied up with what it means to be obedient to the will of the Father. One of the main themes in John's Gospel is precisely that. Mark too insists that Jesus's whole ministry is one of obedience,[9] and certainly the Passion in Mark's Gospel is focused on what it means to do God's will.[10] Abba is the only one to whom he can turn in his agony of fear and indecision. But the Abba relationship does not make things easy for him – on the contrary. In submitting to the Father's will, he submits immediately to the arresting party which comes out of the night. Sonship and servanthood are so close that it is difficult to separate them as they are worked out in Jesus's life; neither are comfortable either for Jesus or for us – but they point the way to the Father and thus to salvation.

It is as we see Jesus's relationship with his Father that we see him coping with other pressures on him and within him. Let us look briefly at some of these.

Guilt

In Luke 2:41–51 we have the incident of Jesus the boy going to Jerusalem with his parents and there remaining to speak with the wise men of Judaism. (A difficult, but no less significant insight than that recorded by Matthew when the wise men came to him.) Picture the agony of distracted and frightened parents, surely quarrelling and blaming each other for losing the boy; their fear giving way to despair and dread, as for three days they tramp the city looking for him. By the time he was found they must have been out of their minds. Guilt is a useless emotion. It paralyses the senses and casts blame on others. It makes it impossible to think clearly or even to think at all and, in the process, blots out almost any other emotion.

It is not surprising therefore that his mother, when she finds him, dumps all her own guilt and anguish on to him. His reaction is not to defend himself, nor to push the blame back on to them, nor to offer some vague excuse: "I thought I had told you that I would be coming here." Rather he accepts the responsibility for his being there by trying to help them see beyond the present situation to his relationship with the Father.

There is a neat irony too in his response to Mary's "Your father and I have been looking for you anxiously": Jesus points beyond Joseph to "Did you not know that I must be in my Father's house?"[11] Again, the Abba relationship is there, strong enough to absorb the guilt and blame and give a new dimension which, by his accepting the responsibility for what he has done, makes it possible to move beyond her guilt. Significantly, Luke comments that he returned to Nazareth with them "and was obedient to them".[12] Sonship, in relation to his earthly parents, can never preclude obedience. While he is under their authority, he is subject to them. It is not surprising that he "increased in wisdom and stature, and in favour with God and man".[13]

Temptation
Jesus's experience of sonship at his baptism gives way to the testing of his new experience in the wilderness. No roseate glow as he moves off into a chorus of Alleluias, with appropriate organ music (or guitars) in the background. No, he is pitched out into the wilderness to be tested. He is indeed full of the Spirit,[14] but that is not enough. Now he is to be subjected to the severe testing which is essential to his ministry. He is on his own – he may have all the angelic powers in heaven available to him, but as he enters the wilderness, Satan's domain, and is tempted, he is again cast back on his Abba relationship. He deals with the temptations by referring to Scripture – but behind this is the solid relationship with the Father, which has been developed by the study of Scripture. Relying on Scripture is not in itself a guarantee against temptation, but relying on Scripture when it reflects a prior

relationship with the Father is at the heart of the Christian response to God. Jesus therefore blocks Sâtan's attack by pointing to the authoritative word of Scripture, which indicates his true relationship with God – the Abba relationship.

So temptation and testing become a means of grace – when they are faced correctly; and for Luke at least, Jesus returns from that experience "in the power of the Spirit".

Fear

There is one particular example of Jesus's fear, to which I have already alluded, namely the agony in the garden.[15] There is little doubt that Jesus was gripped there by a most terrible fear. We seldom see him so obviously and transparently human. The temptation may have tested him, but the agony stretched him almost to breaking point. Again it is to that relationship of intimacy and obedience that he turns and in which he finds the strength to face the concentrated venom of all man's sin. We shall see later that Jesus's injunctions to his disciples to "fear not" came also from that absolute assurance generated by his relationship with the Father.

Shame

Let us take only one, very obvious example of Jesus's shame. At the crucifixion, he was stripped, not to a pair of underpants or even a convenient loincloth. He was naked, and thus shamefully exposed to the ridicule of the crowd. Pinioned as he was, unable even to flick a fly off his face, he was exposed, our naked saviour. The nakedness which is so shameful to men is in fact the same nakedness with which God invests Adam in the garden. And here, he accepts it, and in his doing so, we are enabled to forget the nakedness as we recognise his reliance once again on God. While it is Psalm 22 in which he finds a reflection of his feeling of Godforsakenness, yet even there, we see his dependence on the Father, an expression of "Abba".

At this terrible moment of shame, he seems to accept not

only the shame, but also the responsibility for his condition and, in so doing, absorbs the mockery in such a way that his shame is no more humiliating than any other aspect of his relationship with the Father; it is the way of salvation for sinful man.

Antagonism

If we take the Marcan order of things, Jesus was faced with antagonism from the first day of his ministry. In Luke, he is mobbed and threatened with death as one of the first encounters in his ministry.[16] It seems that it was only the dynamic of his Spirit-filled personality which allowed him to walk through the crowd unharmed as they were about to push him over a cliff. Mark has a build-up to the first great confrontation in Ch. 3:1–6. As a result of this, the Pharisees joined forces with the Herodians to try to "destroy him". For the Pharisees and the Herodians to co-operate in any way indicates a hatred which was so intense that even their traditional rivalry, to say nothing of their theological and political differences, was overcome in the face of the one who was their common enemy. The kingdom of Satan had entered even into the very heart of Jewish leadership.

Such was the hatred they felt towards him, that from the earliest moment of his ministry, the forces of evil were out to destroy him. He was rocking the boat; yet what he was really doing was pulling men back to that point of commitment to God represented in the Law, in Scripture and in his own person. He draws on the Scriptures very frequently in dealing with the antagonism of the religious leaders: "Is it to kill?"[17] In almost all of his use of Scripture he points to himself; when his disciples pluck ears of corn, he retorts, "Have you never read what David did when he was in need and was hungry?"[18] The implication is clear – Jesus is the new David.

It is not necessary to document the antagonism engendered by the last quotation. It is clear that when Jesus was criticised or was faced with antagonism, he used the Scriptures so that the listeners had to make up their minds about him. He did not try to duck what he was doing or evade the (for the Jews) awful implications of his Messiahship and indeed of his relationship with the Father. To forgive sins in his own authority draws attention to himself and to his authority, an authority which the leaders rejected. Yet he stands fast in that authority and the people have to make up their minds about his claims. Even in their antagonism, they cannot avoid him or the claims he makes – claims which spring from a relationship with the Father, which anchors his whole ministry and personality.

Loneliness
One thing that becomes clear when we face Jesus is that he is not afraid to show his feelings. This again springs from the strength of his inner commitment to the Father and his certainty in knowing who he is. So he does not hesitate to show that he is a "loner" when a fervent would-be disciple wants to follow him "wherever you go". Jesus's reply indicates a rejection by society, which any disciple will have to share. "Foxes have holes and birds of the air have nests, but the Son of Man has nowhere to lay his head."[19] That he accepts this state indicates his ability to live with it and overcome what is often the most devastating of human conditions. If we take it further, we see Jesus abandoned by his disciples in the Passion,[20] denied by Peter,[21] and alone and isolated on the Cross.[22]

Apart from that, he was surrounded by the most stolid incomprehension on the part of those closest to him, and even when he tried repeatedly to help them to see, they seemed so blind, deaf or just plain selfish. James and John seem interested only in what they can gain from the situation they are in, rather than in facing with him the mounting forces which are out to destroy him.[23]

At no point do we see Jesus trying to avoid the loneliness. Like all of us, he surely did not desire it, yet he accepted it and made something creative of it, relying on the intimacy of his relationship with the Father.

Anger

For some reason, many Christians have a belief that anger is terribly sinful and must never be shown or expressed. It is probably the most dominant of our emotions and certainly the one which, if suppressed, plays havoc with our lives and attitudes. Yet Jesus is not afraid to show anger on many occasions and is not afraid to take the consequences of his anger. We only have to look at his "cleansing of the Temple".[24] There is here a feeling that he is forcing the issue; if people have taken his triumphant entry into Jerusalem seriously, then they must also take his attitude to the Temple seriously. The anger which has been burning within him erupts as he sees again how the Temple, which represents the presence of God in Israel, is exploited for the profit of those who have influence. There is little doubt that his anger is real and violent – though it expresses itself in his driving out the animals and the money-changers. John, who reflects this incident at the beginning of his Gospel as a sign of the true Israel's advent, nevertheless depicts his anger more ferociously than the synoptic accounts. The anger is focused. It is not a wild lashing out or a dumping of invective on anyone who gets in the way; rather, it burns as a result of men's ability to use the things of God to their own advantage and justify what they do. That is sin, and sin in this context is not to be condoned because of social convention, it is to be recognised and rooted out. It can only be seen for what it is when faced with a force violent enough to disrupt their comfortable extortion of those who are disadvantaged. Notice too, that Jesus's anger is directed against the abuse of "My Father's house", another reference to the Abba relationship. Anger in this way is a necessary force against the insidious inroads of sin; it is neither suppressed, nor general; it does not take the innocent with it, nor does it make apology for itself. It is an instrument of God's fight against sin.

Mark mentions one or two other instances of Jesus's anger – and in each case the anger is focused on the sin or its consequences. So, when he is faced in 3:5 with the hardness of heart of those who were challenging him, he reacts "with anger" (notice in this incident that he is faced with a withered hand which he *can* cure; and withered hearts, which he cannot, because they will not let him near).

So too, when Peter refuses to face the consequences of Jesus's Messiahship, he focuses his anger on Peter in the form of a rebuke, "Get behind me Satan".[25] Anyone who will not accept Jesus, unadorned, is by definition on the side of Satan; to counter the attitude which in effect says, "Don't say that Lord, it is not what we want to hear", must be countered by the sharpness of an anger which cuts through the evasion and faces him with the truth, no matter how painful.

Again, when faced with the duplicity of Herod,[26] he is prepared to take responsibility for calling him a "fox" and he is able to focus his anger even on a ruler who seeks to thwart the kingdom of God.

So it is clear that the anger which bursts from Jesus, comes from the relationship which he has with his father and is used to force people – so anaesthetised by sin that they can neither see it, nor recognise the paralysis which it engenders – to be aware of the demands which Jesus makes.

For Jesus himself, anger is not a sin, it is a proper reaction to those forces which would compromise or pervert the Kingdom of God. These insights into Jesus's feelings have much to teach us as counsellors in our attitudes to our own feelings and emotional responses.

I once heard a talk by Sir Marcus Loane, former Archbishop of Sydney. In all sorts of ways it stirred many thoughts, but one sentence he used has stayed with me. He was talking of the clergy and warned against "the danger of trafficking in unfelt truths". Recently a neighbour, hearing that I was a minister, came to talk to me about the problems related to her husband's retirement and their marriage. She asked if I had ever had to deal with anything like it before. I said that I had never either had to face the problems she described, nor come across anyone else who had. I said I was prepared to listen to her, but I would not be able to do anything more than go along with her feelings and try to hear what she was saying. I am not sure how effective or helpful that was, but she was able to talk at great length and possibly felt better for it. *I* learned a great deal, but cannot say that I could identify with most of her feelings. Those that I could identify with rang bells, but not in such a way that I was able to help her much with her problems. The point is, it is dishonest to try to say that one is aware of feelings, when one is not. It is better to admit that we are not where the person is and take it from there if they want to go further.

Jesus experienced all of the feelings which any of us are likely to face and made something of them; coping with the whole range of human emotion and condition, strong in his primary relationship and strong in his awareness of who he was. He used the title "Son of Man" of himself and gave it new value. He declared stunning truths about himself in the sure knowledge that "I and the Father are one"[27] and so the great "I am" sayings of John's Gospel erupt into a shattered world with life and world-changing force. Because he *knows* Abba, he is able to know himself and stand firm in the authority which this self-knowledge gives.

The counsellor, if he is to be effective, is to have something of that relationship with the Father. The New Testament makes it clear that we through the saving work of Jesus, and in the power of the Spirit of God, are also able to call him Abba; Paul's incredible eighth chapter of Romans makes it clear that we are heirs to the wealth of God's riches and, as heirs, we are sons led by the Spirit of God, who lives in us, and in the cry "Abba, Father" we give testimony to our new status in Christ. It is a marvellous thing to realise that we have available to us the same relationship with the Father that Jesus had, "provided", says Paul, "we suffer with him . . . we may also be glorified with him".[28] There's the rub for those of us who are called to the counselling ministry. When the suffering is not there, we traffic in unfelt truths. We know neither the suffering, nor the consequent glory.

If we are to take the counselling ministry seriously it means, more than anything else, that we take ourselves seriously. And that involves the rather horrifying task of facing up to ourselves; of hearing what others say of us; of seeing ourselves as others see us; of recognising our pride, our bombast, our angers, our areas of temptation, our fears, our inadequacies, our lonelinesses, and our terrifying inability to communicate anything other than our own sin.

During one of the first lectures I attended on counselling, a member of the class asked the professor if he thought we all ought to be subjected to psychoanalysis. The professor's answer was revealing. He said he believed we ought, because if we were to be good counsellors, we should know at least one person very well indeed: "And who better than the person for whom you have an abiding and deeply rooted fascination, namely, yourself?"

Now, for the record, I did not undergo such a process of psychoanalysis, and I did not specially respond to his style of teaching. For me, it was too humanly based and, with Jay Adams, I believe that is not where the Christian counsellor should start.[29] But I do agree that it is an absolute essential for the counsellor to know himself well and have no illusions about himself. I have come across too many counsellors, especially if they are ordained, who are so busy giving of themselves all the time, that they are terribly threatened by receiving counselling, as though, somehow, for them, it would be a sign of weakness or incompetence. But we must be dependent and know ourselves so that we may never "traffic in unfelt truths". To know oneself is also to know the possibility of coming to the Father, of being able, in humility and dependence, to call him Abba, and to derive from that relationship the authority which God gives us as his sons and heirs.

Thus, the counsellor has to battle through the issues of his life – in the silence of prayer, where the water of the Spirit may flow or may dry up. He is to agonise with his clients, he is to be prepared to listen to them and willing to hear. He is to stop his activity long enough to study the Scriptures and to make them his own, that the words are vehicles for the primary relationship with the Father, whereby, in the Spirit, *we* are able to call him Abba.

I am not suggesting something either easy or glib. It is a lifelong task, of humiliations and failures, of pride bubbling up almost unrecognised, which has to be seen and rooted out, so that once more our dependency on God may be re-established. We will hear the siren voice of people telling us how wonderful we are, and we will believe them, because we want to. We will think that *we* are the counsellor, forgetting that the Holy Spirit alone is the counsellor and all we are are agents whereby he may enter into others and help them deal with their problems. We will again and again come back to Abba and know his love and the joy of doing his will and, as we pray, we will know that praise, antagonism and criticism, are all unusually appalling half-truths, which mean nothing, unless they are filtered through the fine mesh of our relationship with God.

It is difficult to tell others how to pray. Two books, however, have been incredibly helpful to me. Henri J. Nouwens', *Reaching out* (Fount) and Thomas J. Green's, *When the Well Runs Dry* (Ave Maria Press 1979) are both marvellous for helping us to take silence seriously. In my experience, it is as I have learned to be quiet, in the presence of the Spirit of God, that I have been able to catch a glimpse of myself and pick up a flicker of an idea of what it means to know Abba. Strangely, for me, it is both an intimate and joyful relationship, as well as something so indefinably mysterious, that all I can do is be silent and know that he is God. I am aware that all that I know of myself, God knows better, and all that I have undergone (for me, loneliness in one particular form, and anger in many forms have been my main problems), no matter how small and how inconsequential they may be, are nevertheless areas where Jesus has also been. And as I experience the pages of the Gospels, he comes to me and shows me, not so much how to understand them, but how to accept and face them in the loving presence of Abba, Father.

Chapter
2

Listening – and its problems

Listening is both gift and acquired skill; it derives from a
loving concern for the other, from a lack of self-consciousness
on the part of the counsellor, and a refusal to inject one's own
experience into the situation in such a way that the direction
of the interview focuses on the counsellor, rather than the
counsellee.

Having said that, listening involves more than words.
Contrary to Jay Adams's insistence,[1] listening *must* try to
hear feelings, for whether we like it or not, we act more on
feelings than we do on thought. Feelings get in the way in
relationships and one of the counsellor's responsibilities is to
help the person past the feelings to the reality of the situation.
So listening hears the feelings behind the words, it takes them
seriously, but does not allow them to be the only motivating
force in a person's life. Listening too focuses all one's attention on the person, it hears the evasions and inconsistencies,
the illogicalities and fears, the likes and dislikes; and in the
process, it starts to help the counsellor to see the other person
as he really is – and to love him for what he is, rather than
what he would like to be or thinks he is.

Counselling founders on bad listening more than anything
else – professional counsellors are not necessarily good
listeners. I have heard tapes of one of the most popular
counsellors I know, who seems never to allow a person to
finish a sentence before telling him what is wrong. The fact
that he is popular means that there are people who need
to be told what to do and be. My worry is how much he

misses by not listening, no matter how much experience he has.

My own listening ability needs continually to be disciplined. I can remember an occasion when, having heard an address which I had given on listening, a friend wanted to speak to me about a matter which was very important to him. After about ten minutes, I looked at my watch, at which point he stopped talking and within a short time, left. No amount of assurance could persuade him that I had in fact been interested in what he was saying. What I had done spoke more loudly than the words I was using. That he is still my friend says more about his charity than my concern.

I have discovered many ways in which listening is impaired and most of them involve too much self and too little care of the other. So, to look at one's watch communicates that one is more worried about time than the person. If we do have a time bind, we must say so and find a more suitable time when we can concentrate completely. No one that I have known believes that that is unloving or unconcerned.

Then there have been times when I have been so tired that it is physically impossible to listen adequately. One is so busy trying to stay awake! It is more loving in that context to reschedule the appointment than to go through with what can only be a masquerade.

A worse fault is sitting listening to a person for whom one does not really care at all. Indifference is a terrible sin – it is pride gone mad, to the point that it abandons care and immerses the counsellor in himself. If a person does not care, he must never counsel, for by definition he will be unable to listen.

Listening involves one's whole being and primarily the specific faculties of hearing and sight; the spiritual gifts of discernment and knowledge are essential too. So body language – observation of how the person sits, how he holds himself, nervous habits – is all part of hearing. And discernment and knowledge are gifts more intuitive than deductive, though both are based on observation and listening. They are gifts of the Spirit, which are part of God's equipment for the counsellor. If we are not prepared to listen with all of the gifts God has given us, it is unlikely that we will hear what is really being said.

Listening also involves a relationship. The counsellor cannot believe that he will go into a counselling relationship and remain unchanged. If he does, he is not counselling – for where there is no relationship, the counsellor is no more than a talking block. We shall look in a later chapter at Jesus's exercise of compassion, an essential ingredient for any counselling relationship. Having seen some of the problems and pitfalls of listening, let us look at how Jesus listened.

Jesus's listening

There are two striking episodes in Mark's Gospel which give us the first clues as to the nature of Jesus's listening; in both cases, the insights into his listening are secondary to the main thrust of the episode – thus we are able to perceive the listening in its proper context.

Mark 10:46–52   Blind Bartimaeus

The context here is crucial. The whole of Chapter 10 is concerned with different aspects of the nature of discipleship and commitment. And now, as he is about to enter Jerusalem, there to make his final play for recognition as Messiah on his own terms, he heals a blind beggar. I have little doubt that Mark sees in Bartimaeus a sign for all who would follow Jesus. We, too, are blind beggars, in sharp contrast to the way in which James and John have seen themselves in the previous incident.[2] More than anything, Jesus needs people who can see and follow him "on the way". (The Way is one of the oldest names given to the Church, and is used here deliberately to show *how* we are to follow Jesus.)

Jesus has come out of Jericho, surrounded by a crowd of enthusiastic followers. The plight of Bartimaeus is far from their thoughts or even their interests. On hearing Bartimaeus's calls for help – increased in proportion to the crowd's attempts to stop him shouting – *Jesus stops*.[3] And here is the first insight into his listening. He stops and focuses on the one person whom the crowd has no hesitation in either avoiding or abandoning; one who recognises his own need and Jesus's power. So *Jesus stops*. He is neither too busy, *nor too popular* to stop and listen. Next, he makes the beggar come to him.[4] The beggar has to move to him and even then *Jesus presupposes nothing*. Obviously, he can see that the beggar is blind. Clearly that is the area in which he needs help, yet Jesus first listens to what the blind man says – even when he must have assumed that he knew the answer. His question to Bartimaeus is not, therefore, rhetoric. It is *taking the other person seriously* and allowing him the *freedom both to know and state his problem* in his own way and with his own insights. Only then, after Bartimaeus has given his side of things, does Jesus act, for the blind man's salvation and to Jesus's glory. Notice that it requires faith on the part of the blind man – a trust that Jesus can and will act for his salvation.

Mark 5:25–34　*The woman with a flow of blood*

Again, the context is important. Jesus has just healed the man with the legion of demons,[5] to the fear and astonishment of the local townsfolk. He is then approached by Jairus to heal his daughter[6] and, on the way, almost mobbed by the crowd, certainly jostled by many (probably those who were fascinated by Jesus and wanted to see whether he would be able to heal the little girl). Jesus perceived "in Himself that power had gone forth from Him".[7] The build-up to this incident is a desperate woman, subject to the ministrations of the medical profession, none of whom, with all their skill, or lack of it, could cure her. Now, impoverished, desperate and probably fearful, she *risks herself* by simply touching his garments. It is the risk of faith to which Jesus responds, and Mark reports that while the haemorrhage dried up in her, Jesus perceived that the power for healing had gone from him. It is this perception which is at the heart of his awareness and there are many times when Jesus perceives, be it the power here, or the hardness of heart of the Pharisees[8] and it is that insight which makes the difference. The word used in the Greek on both of these occasions means something like knowing through and through, or even recognising. Essentially it is the process of discernment, the ability to see beyond the obvious to the reality of the situation.

Notice that Jesus stopped here also. He "turned about" and with the crowd jostling him, he was still able to perceive the real need and act of faith in a sea of want. Even with the urgency of the call to get to Jairus's daughter, he had time to stop and recognise the woman's faith and, in that moment, to hear a cry more muted than the crowd's, yet deeper than their often profound needs.

We will look in more detail at what we can learn from Jesus in those incidents later in the chapter; but let us look at other aspects of his listening, in slightly less detail.

John's Gospel

"Hearing" is a central theme in John's Gospel. The discourses on hearing in Chapters 5 and 8 are central to the teaching of the Gospel. In each of these cases, the listener is not Jesus, but those to whom Jesus is communicating. The implication of much of this is that they are either antagonistic to Jesus, or so preoccupied with "the world" that they cannot hear. At the same time, if they do hear, they will receive eternal life. In many ways, this is summed up by Peter. At the end of Chapter 6, after Jesus's teaching on the Bread of Life, many of his disciples abandoned him because they said, "This is a hard saying; who can listen to it?"[9] Jesus turns to the twelve and asks if they too, will abandon him, and to this question Peter's response is the core of the followers' attitude to Jesus. "Lord, to whom shall we go? You have the words of eternal life; and we have believed and have come to know that you are the Holy One of God."[10]

This is the responsive hearing of the Word – hearing the teaching not only of Jesus the man but of the eternal Logos, the Word made flesh. It is the recognition of Jesus as the Word, which brings life and gives the Spirit. I am not seeking to deny the importance of that hearing – if anything, that is the hearing of the one who is counselled, the one who, as he hears the Word and responds, enters eternal life. That, if you like, is the aim of counselling, and is crucial to the whole process.

But what we are more concerned with here is the quality of Jesus's listening and there are one or two incidents in John's Gospel which help us. The most obvious is the incident involving the Samaritan woman.[11] This, too, is a time for stopping[12] and it is also a time when Jesus breaks convention by talking to a much despised Samaritan, and a Samaritan *woman* at that. What starts as a simple request for water ends with the woman saying to those who come from the city, "He told me all that ever I did."[13] In the process, Jesus not only listens to her words, but perceives that behind her somewhat brash attitude lies a deep inadequacy, an inability to relate, so that already she has had more husbands than she needs. The last husband cannot even be described as a husband.

Jesus's listening here can be described as "perception" or some would call it "a word of knowledge". Whatever it is, it goes beyond the externals to the heart of the problem – in this case, an inability to be committed to one person for any length of time. So the drabness and apparent uselessness of her life is pierced by Jesus's insight and this opens the way for a new set of values and a new way of life and of looking at herself.

Jesus's conversation with Nicodemus[14] is equally revealing of his listening abilities. Mostly, of course, we focus, as we read this passage, on the profundity of the teaching, especially as it is aimed at a representative of the unredeemed Israel. This interview starts with Nicodemus making compliments,[15] but that is not where Jesus is, or what he needs. Nicodemus is faced with a truth which he cannot understand and every time he takes it literally, Jesus hears not only the incomprehension, but also the defensiveness. It is almost as though Nicodemus does not want to hear things beyond his comprehension, or outside his own traditional ways of looking at things. Yet Jesus hears the fear, hears the fascination too and pushes through to a different set of conclusions than those represented by Nicodemus. The last verse in this section gives Nicodemus his clue: "he who does what is true comes to the light, that it may be clearly seen that his deeds have been wrought in God."[16] So, in a very different style of listening, Jesus hears Nicodemus and points him in the direction of salvation.

Jesus's listening to Nicodemus had another effect as well. Because Jesus really heard Nicodemus, he made it possible for Nicodemus to hear him and that was in fact far more important for Nicodemus than he imagined. Jesus has the words of salvation and by taking Nicodemus seriously, he frees Nicodemus to hear those words and be saved. It is not surprising that later in the Gospel Nicodemus is reported as insisting that under the law Jesus should get a fair hearing.[17]

Other aspects of Jesus's listening

One of the most important aspects of Jesus's listening, is his ability to *hear the sin and inconsistencies* in situations. Thus, when the Pharisees try to trap him by asking about Sabbath observance[18] in the Matthean parallel to Mark 3:1–6, Jesus recognises the inconsistency of their argument; a sheep is of greater value than a person. So, too, when they try to trick him with questions about the law and tradition[19] he is able to hear the inconsistencies and hypocrisy which convince and confuse others and reveals those pieties for the sham that they are. Likewise, the question relating to allegiance to Caesar and the problem of tax payment is heard as a trap and again he asks the question which points to the right perspective.[20] It is scarcely surprising therefore that he warns his disciples against the "leaven of the Pharisees".[21] Leaven in this context, as in almost every other, implies an evil influence. Leaven permeates the dough, giving it its taste and lightness, but it is also the substance which makes the bread go sour. It is thus seen in ancient Israel and here in Jesus's teaching as an influence to be avoided. The Pharisees had an ability to pervert the truth in order to maintain their own ends at any cost, or, as they would see it, the traditions of Israel as worked out from the Law. Jesus was a threat to them precisely because he heard their inconsistencies and hypocrisies and revealed them for what they were.

Faith, too, is the object of Jesus's hearing. Thus, he hears the centurion[22] – a Roman, whose recognition of Jesus's authority was such that he could turn to him in trust. The faith is transmitted in terms of the centurion's perception of Jesus as well as within the centurion's own context, and as a result, Jesus is able to heal the servant. While others heard the words, Jesus heard the faith. The same is true of the Syro-Phoenician woman.[23] What some might have interpreted as impudence or simply quick thinking, is heard by Jesus for what it is – a communication of faith, which is the first step towards healing and salvation.

Jesus's listening leads to change

It is obvious that in almost every instance I have cited, the person who is heard by Jesus enters into the way of salvation – into the Kingdom of God. Jesus's ability to hear the faith, hear what is actually being communicated through words and actions, is the key to their new life. But the other side must not be forgotten. It is Jesus too who, in entering into the re-lationships, is himself more complete. This must, to some extent, be conjectured, though we see how, after the Samaritan woman had told the rest of the town about him, he and his disciples stayed with them for two more days. Surely, it was their acceptance of him, the relationship which it created, as well as their desire to want to hear him, which made it possible for him to give of himself in so radical a way.

So often Jesus is surrounded by people who cling to him, yet also build him up. Thus, Peter's confession is a golden moment for Jesus, as he is at last seen for who he is, even though the triumph is short-lived. There seems, at least in Matthew,[24] a sense in which Jesus himself is fulfilled, there is an intimacy and a joyfulness which gives us a glimpse into Jesus's own needs.

More often, it is Jesus's preparedness to take the other person seriously, to be deeply affected by the situation, which makes the change. The sight of Jesus weeping over Jerusalem,[25] weeping at the misery of Martha and Mary at the death of Lazarus,[26] being deeply moved by the condition of those around him,[27] or the condition of a leper,[28] or "marvelling at their unbelief",[29] makes us aware of his own readiness to become emotionally involved in the affairs of those around him. And it is that preparedness to show his own emotion, which is part of the process of bringing people into the Kingdom of God.

The prayer of Jesus

We will say more of Jesus's praying later, but one element of it must be emphasised here. There are several occasions when Jesus is recorded as having gone off by himself to pray; there is one instance, however, when it gives rise to quite specific action. Luke tells us (in contrast to Matthew and Mark, who do not mention this particular aspect) that Jesus went "into the hills to pray and all night he continued in prayer to God".[30] The result of that night of prayer was that he received guidance as to whom he should appoint as Apostles. Quite simply, Jesus listened to God and received the necessary guidance. Thus, Jesus's listening is a two-way thing – *it goes out towards people and it constantly turns back to the Father.* Without both activities, Jesus would not have been able to achieve the will of the Father.

For the counsellor, there is much to learn from Jesus's listening. Perhaps we should start with the last point – prayer. One of the best descriptions of prayer which I have come across was given me by a friend while I was in training for the ministry: "kneel down and shut up." That is a good definition for, if we learn the gift of silence, we may hear what the Father has for us. If the counsellor does not develop the gift of silence, then the chances are that he will not hear the Lord God – and will start depending on his own insights and abilities. That would be sad, because then he will fail those who come to him seeking help. There are certain clear insights about listening, which we can learn from Jesus. *We have got to stop in order to listen clearly.* A friend of mine once went to see his bishop, who carried on writing a letter throughout the interview. It did not matter whether the bishop got it right or wrong afterwards – my friend believed the bishop was not listening and shortly after the interview he resigned from the diocese. So many of us, especially if we are in the ministry, believe that we are too busy to stop and listen, so we never really hear and we are not much use to those who come to us.

As a boy about to leave school, I believed that God was calling me to the ministry and I went to see Father Trevor Huddleston about it. At the time, he was possibly the most hated *and* the most loved man in the country and, when I arrived at the Priory at Rosettenville for my appointment, I found a message asking me to wait as he had been delayed. Throughout the morning messages kept coming and I waited three hours for him to appear. When he came he apologised and then for the next hour or so I was the only person in his life. All his faculties were focused on me, he listened with his whole being and when he spoke, it was finally to work out with me a plan of action. I went away with an awareness that I had been in the presence (again) of a man of God, whose every resource was available to me. It was only the next day that I read in the newspapers that he had been involved in a confrontation with the police. So involved was he with me, that I do not believe it occurred to him to tell me of *his* problems, which made mine totally insignificant by comparison.

Stopping is essential to listening – and that may mean anywhere, be it in the town, in a supermarket, while writing a sermon – it can be anywhere and anytime. When the person tugs your sleeve, for God's sake, stop and listen with all the resources God has given you.

When you stop, listen and don't think you have the answer
All of us have had the experience of trying to pour out our troubles when we are cut short and the counsellor launches into an impassioned digression, which has nothing to do with what we are trying to say. It is frustrating and draws more attention to the counsellor than the client. How often have I not seen a look of anger, bewilderment or even boredom as I talk, assuming that I know the answer before the problem has even been stated. Jesus gave the person every opportunity to state the problem, and to do it in his way and in his time. There is no sense of the people with whom Jesus made contact being pushed – he listened until he heard clearly, and *then* he spoke.

Listening involves perception and discernment
I have previously in this chapter disagreed with Jay Adams when he believes that the counsellor's job is not to listen to feelings. He believes we must hear the words only, define the issue and then take action.[31] Of course we must listen for the feelings; and the process of reflecting them back to the counsellee may be the best way of helping him see what he is actually feeling. If, however, we do no more than reflect back the feelings, then I would want to agree with Adams that more needs to happen; clearly the person does *not* always have the necessary resources within himself to try new ways of living. Any real listening involves going beyond feelings, to actions and reactions long since forgotten or repressed. Here is where true listening comes into play – to perceive that there *is* something beyond the feelings (*when* there is) and to help the person to the more fearful consequences of facing up to those areas of dread. Perception – and the word of knowledge – are spiritual gifts, for which we must pray. I have no doubt that the Spirit of God gives them to us as we need them.

My own experience is that they are not automatic gifts. Each time we come to a dead end in counselling, we have to agonise through that with the Lord, and he gives us the way through to the heart of the problem, often in ways which are surprising and unexpected.

Listening involves hearing the inconsistencies and omissions
The counsellor will train himself to hear what is *not* said, just as much as what *is* said. On one occasion a man came to see me about his problems and throughout insisted on what a wonderful woman his wife was and how much he loved her. That did not somehow tie in with the rest of what he was saying, but I let it pass for the time and then right at the end of the interview, I rather offhandedly threw in a comment about his wife. To his astonishment, for he was unguarded, he referred to her as "that bitch", after which the real issues started to emerge. If a person does *not* talk about an obvious member of his family, or emphasises one to the virtual omission of the others, there is a good chance he may be avoiding an issue. It is worth at least noting for future reference.

Listen for true faith
True faith does not always sound like it. Often a person will come up with many of the clichés and jargon of religious language. It will sound impressive, but it may well be part of a well built camouflage – just as it may be a genuine desire to come to the Lord. But it may not add up to the reality of that person's life. Yet if you listen clearly, you will perceive a real nugget of faith and you will know it as the basis on which new life can be built and new hopes established.

On other occasions, you will be listening for religious language and not hear the faith, couched perhaps in such everyday terms that it may easily be missed. It may be in the asking of a very ordinary question which gets to the centre of a problem; it may be the person's exercise of extraordinary patience, humility and love which, because they are extraordinary, could easily be lost because we are not expecting to hear them. The point is clear: expect to hear the unexpected and it is remarkable what you will hear.

Listening may change your life

Listening is a dangerous activity – for you will enter, by dint of listening, into a relationship with another, which will affect you emotionally and draw you into his life, thought patterns, values and aspirations. If the Holy Spirit is present, which you must pray for and assume, then it is the Spirit working in you and the other person which will effect the change. I am not saying you will agree with all that the other person is, but you will be drawn to him. I am not saying, either, that you should be so drawn in that you take his side, or see things only from his point of view. Then you become part of the problem and that is useless. But to weep and laugh, to exercise compassion and love, to allow dependencies in the process of helping people to live again, that is at least part of counselling and part of being used in the way of salvation.

Listening frees the other to listen

Some while ago I had a most difficult person to counsel. He wanted help, but only on his terms. That he was a very sick person and that I was the only person he would speak to did not seem to matter. He was not prepared to accept anything which he did not want. His stubborn pride refused to see his illness as serious and that his illness was related to his refusal to hear and accept was obvious to all: medical doctor, parents, teachers and friends. Because I was one of the few to whom he would speak, I had to find a way past the impasse. For many hours I listened carefully and with as much love as he would allow me to show. Finally I felt I had to say to him that it was in his disobedience alone which lay his ongoing sickness. Of course behind the disobedience were many fears which he could not and did not want to face, but because I had taken him seriously, it had actually freed him to start listening to me – and others – and ultimately to Our Lord. On that road alone lay the path to recuperation.

Listening is a gift of the Spirit

Listening is related to gentleness and pastoring, to meekness and to prophecy, to patience and to the gift of teaching. You cannot avoid it, but you had better start praying for it. And the best way to start praying for it, is to kneel down and shut up!

Chapter
3

Fear

Fear is at the heart of the sinful human condition. The fear expressed in Genesis 3 is the fear of being seen for what we are. That is a fear of exposure, a feeling of shame and the fear that that shame may lead to derision from others.

I have come to the conclusion that almost all of the problems I have had to deal with in counselling have had their origins in feelings of shame, rejection and humiliation. It is also true that those agonies are so strong for most of us that the fear of having to face them again is enough to change the direction of our lives; as far as it is possible for us to organise ourselves, we will avoid the situations which cause the shame, or rejection. Fear, or dread, as many would have it, is the most powerful motivating force and is always close to the surface of our lives and reactions. It is at the heart of sin, for it draws us away from God, and focuses us on ourselves.

What is fear?

The biblical concept of fear varies. On the one hand, it has a strong sense of the awefulness of God: fear of God is the basis of all worship; it is the beginning of wisdom; it is the wonder which comes from being aware of the magnitude and presence of a loving, judging and yet infinitely trustworthy God. Psalm 8 – one of the most profoundly moving in the whole Psalter – captures something of the wonder of God; loving and yet aweful in majesty. That sense of wonder and awe would be described as "fear". That fear is life-giving, for it pulls our attention to God and is thus the reversal of sin. Fear of God in that context puts God back into the centre of things, as far as man's response is concerned and that denies the power of sin and Satan.

Fear for most of us is something very different; it is that state of being, be it temporary or permanent, which so fixes on anything which in some way threatens to destroy, or which it is supposed will destroy us, that we cannot avoid being obsessed by it. If that is a working definition of fear, it is at once clear that, by drawing our attention away from God, it is very much the essence of sin. Very frequently, when people are caught in the grip of fear, they will turn to God, not as a free response to him, but in an attempt to gain security and somehow deflect that which they fear. At the centre of fear is the obsession in some way or another with destruction – again in a variety of forms; it may be the threat of the destruction of my land, my values, commitments, property, family or self – or all of them!

So let us look at some of the fears which dominate most of us. Probably the most powerful is the fear of death. I am not sure which aspect of death is most dominant, though as I look at myself, I suppose it is the fear of losing all that I am, facing up to my own finitude, my own dependence and having to accept that I cannot really control my life. It is a fear of moving to nothingness, of ultimately being forgotten, and Sheol is the place where God has forgotten those who have died. *That* is total death, where not even God remembers, and of all things it is truly terrifying. That is what our Lord means when he tells us to fear them who can kill body and spirit in hell,[1] for then there is nothing more to save.

There is another aspect of fear too – what Frank Lake calls *primal pain*, the distress, rejection or trauma which affects the foetus in the womb. Lake's insistence that the reactions of the mother during the first trimester of pregnancy affect the child's sense of acceptance or rejection, is in my opinion not only wholly biblical – one only has to look at two people such as Jeremiah[2] and Paul[3] to be aware of a sense of God's involvement with them in the womb and before – but it has been borne out in my own experience of counselling.[4] I have counselled a person who believed that his mother had never wanted him and who knew this long before he was born. On checking out with his mother, he discovered that she had resented him from the moment she knew she was pregnant, and certainly had not wanted the baby EVER! Later assurances of love did nothing to remove the sense of rejection imprinted in that first agonising awareness.

The primal pain is often the most profound sense of rejection. It shows that as others are caught in the web of sin, the child cannot help being rejected, but lives with the awful consequences. The most fascinating case study I have come across is "Dibs",[5] who must have been the victim of such feelings on the part of his mother and certainly of his father, and I have no doubt – though this is not mentioned in the book – that he was thus affected.[6] It is as interesting to see how Dibs's father was acutely embarrassed by anything which was in any sense "childish" or "beneath him", and his embarrassment took its toll on Dibs.[7] So again, fear is the *fear of being rendered a nobody in the eyes of others* – a fool, a laughing stock – these are the frightening words, reflecting situations to be avoided. So fear acts as a constant goad, for at another level it involves a lack of trust, primarily of self and therefore of others and of course ultimately of God, and that creates distortions or exaggerations of the truth.

The biblical picture of chaos

The Old Testament has two pictures of chaos, which are taken over and used in the New. The first of these is the picture of a watery abyss, or deep, "without form and void".[8] It is a common picture used in many forms. The Red Sea is parted and the "deeps congealed in the heart of the sea".[9] The waters of destruction mount in the time of Noah,[10] so that only Noah and those in the ark are spared. The image of chaos in this form is used repeatedly in the Psalms.

Frequently this imagery describes the personal sense of helplessness in the face of the forces of chaos which are consuming the writer.[11] Thus in one of my other favourite Psalms:

> Save me, O God,
> For the waters have come up to my neck
> I sink in deep mire
> Where there is no foothold;
> I have come into deep waters,
> And the flood sweeps over me.[12]

The Psalmist may feel he is drowning, but in fact the waters of chaos are "those who hate me without cause . . . who would destroy me . . . who attack me with lies".[13] The forces of chaos which he has to face are all too human, and it is in the light of those attacks, that he turns to God as the only one who has power to overcome them.

Chaos is seen in the powers which we fear, for they seek to destroy even that which is of God. No wonder Satan is very quickly associated with the watery deep – and no wonder in the vision of the new heaven and a new earth "the sea was no more",[14] for the watery abyss has finally been overcome. The forces of chaos which seek to destroy God's people have themselves been conquered.

The other image of chaos presented in the Old Testament is that of desert – a waterless waste. Thus, creation is described as the process of God watering the earth and making man. Prior to that "no plant of the field was yet in the earth and no herb of the field had yet sprung up – for the Lord God had not caused it to rain on the earth."[15] Dust is very quickly the symbol of death – "you are dust, and to dust you shall return"[16] and that too reflects in other areas of the Old Testament. So in Psalm 22: "my strength is dried up like a potsherd and my tongue cleaves to my jaws; thou dost lay me in the dust of death."[17] The wilderness is therefore a place of dust, which does not support life.[18] Unless God acts, there is no water and therefore no food. The point of the forty years in the wilderness is that, in spite of the question "can God spread a table in the wilderness?",[19] he did just that, and sustained them in the place which of itself could not provide sustenance. So we are again only one step away from the idea that the wilderness is the home of Satan. It is implied in the Gospels[20] and is described as the place for evil spirits in Matthew's Gospel.[21] It is Satan's domain.

We should note here that the Jews believed that God had tamed the forces of chaos at creation; these forces had gradually, through the inroads of sin, won back areas of creation, which themselves have to be won back before the Kingdom of God can be finally ushered in. The power of the evil one, Satan, is therefore associated with chaos, for chaos does not support the life-giving creativity of God, which Satan actively opposes.

Jesus and the forces of chaos and evil

Jesus attacks Satan on his home ground, at the very start of his mission,[22] when he enters the wilderness for that purpose. From then on, he is engaged in a life and death struggle of cosmic proportions on several fronts. We see him locked in battle with demons; with sickness, most crucially with paralysis and leprosy; with the hardness of heart of the religious leaders; with the forces of chaos in the form of wind, sea, and desert; with the fear of death and with death itself, in others and in relation to himself.[23] The point about all these instances is that, in some way or another, fear is at the root of them, to say nothing of the fear they engendered. It is true that in the course of time, at least some aspects of chaos and evil had come to be accepted with a reasonable degree of comfort. So it was only when the man with a legion of demons in him was "clothed and in his right mind" that the local townspeople were afraid,[24] presumably because they were suddenly aware of a much greater power than they had experienced before and did not know what to do in the face of such power; it had disturbed the equilibrium to which they had become accustomed.

Wherever Jesus confronts the forces which create fear by threatening to destroy, he exercises an authority, which *we can only describe in terms of his person*. He is recognised by an evil spirit and named "The holy one of God". Jesus rebukes the evil spirit and commands him to "be silent and come out".[25] The demon knows his enemy, even when the crowd do not know their saviour, and Jesus exercises the authority vested in himself in such a way that the unclean spirit has to obey. This same sense of Jesus as master over the forces of evil and chaos is in all the confrontations in the Gospels.

Thus, when the disciples, terrified at the storm which threatens to sink their boat and drown them,[26] turn to Jesus, he rebukes the wind and the sea. It is the same word used when he rebukes the demon, and the authority is unquestionable. In this incident there are two elements which are the key to our understanding of Jesus and his authority in our counselling. The first is that while the sea raged, Jesus slept. I have no doubt that Jesus's sleep is the sign of his absolute authority over the chaotic forces around them and that Jesus's sleep is the sign for men to exercise faith. As Lord of Creation, he cannot be overcome by chaos and so, in spite of the fear of his disciples, experienced sailors many of them, that they would perish, his sleep is the sign by which they can have trust, even in the face of the most terrifying forces. The implications for counselling are enormous and we will look at them later.

The second is that Jesus contrasts faith with fear – or, in this case,[27] cowardice. Thus faith is reliance on Jesus, the Lord of Creation; and fear neither recognises his authority, nor believes that he can in fact save. So faith or belief is one of the counters to fear, though it is always faith *in* Jesus or the power of God. This is true in several other situations. When Jesus arrives at Jairus's house and faces the news that the child is dead, he tells them "do not fear, only believe".[28] Later, when he declares that the child is asleep (a hint of his own sleep in the boat?), he is met by laughter, which would surely

be the expression of total disbelief. Again, faith is the antidote to fear.

At the Garden of Gethsemane, when Jesus faces his own
fear, it is the absolute trust in the Father and preparedness to
do his will, come what may, which gives him release from the
torment of fear, even if it does not make his life any easier. In
fact, one of the problems with the Christian faith is precisely
that. *Life does not become easy when we believe*, it is just that
we have the resources in Jesus and in the power of the Spirit,
to go forward with greater power than that of the fear which
causes us to hold back.

Probably the most powerful incident involving the fear of
the disciples is that of Jesus walking on the water.[29] After the
feeding of the five thousand, Jesus (as is so often the case after
expending himself in intensive ministry) goes off alone to
pray. So, separated from his disciples, he comes to them in the
dark and on the sea blown by the wind. In the face of the
chaotic forces and the apparition on the water, they are
"terrified", which is hardly surprising. These primal forces of
destruction are again put into perspective when Jesus tells the
disciples to be confident, or have courage, and then uses the
key words, "It is I. Do not be afraid." The Greek is very
dramatic, for *ego eimi* here are the words used to denote the
Holy Name of God in the Septuagint. So, Jesus again affirms
that there is no possibility of fear when he, the Lord of chaos,
is present. The peace which follows is that peace which comes
from his dominant authority over the forces which assert a
destructive power in the lives of men. So here faith is focused
not simply on Jesus the man but on God Incarnate, who casts
out fear. The answer to fear is trust in God; he is utterly
reliable and actively involved in destroying the forces which
make for fear. So it is in every part of his ministry; he orders
the leprosy to go away because he wills it and he shows that
these forces, terrifying though they may be, are not as terrifying as we think.

This is brought home most vividly in the raising of
Lazarus.[30] The declaration that Lazarus has died so that they

may believe, gives way to the declaration, "I am the Resurrection and the Life." "I am" is the divine word of self revelation, the "I am" who is the Lord of history and covenant, of creation and life. Here the "I am" is directly contrasted with the death which we all face, death which brings grief and agony to Lazarus's sisters and friends. But God's answer cuts right through death to resurrection and new life, and that life is the life of God. It is God's answer to the fearful forces of death and shows the glory which is God's alone. So while he is deeply moved by the plight of the sisters, yet the answer to the powers of death, as indeed to every other power which thwarts God's creativity and life-giving presence, is "I am": the divine presence in the midst of chaos, however it may come to us.

Thus all of the "I am" sayings are intended to declare the saving presence of God in every facet of life, and to show the direction for us to move. It is life and light, as the darkness seeks to quench the light. But "the light shines in the darkness and the darkness has not overcome it".[31]

So we see that in Jesus's actions in the face of fear he draws attention to his own person and authority, making it thus possible to fear God, and as a result, to fear nothing else. The sense of fear, which follows the stilling of the storm,[32] is the same which follows a mighty act of God, and that is the creative fear to which he leads us. Perhaps what the Gospels are saying is something like this: Fear God, worship him with awe and thanksgiving, and there will be nothing else to fear. It is beautifully expressed in one of my favourite hymns:

> Fear Him, ye saints, and you will then
> Have nothing else to fear;
> Make you His service your delight,
> Your want shall be His care.[33]

The counsellor will always come up against fear; it is there in some form or another in almost every counselling situation. As I think back over my counselling experience, it spreads insidiously to almost every part of life. The mother, fearful of the rebellion of her child; the husband or wife fearful of losing a partner; the adulterer fearful of being discovered; the person who dislikes himself, fearful that others will see him as he really is; the liar who is covering a sin of some sort; the person fearful of not having enough money. So we go on. The rejected person, fearful that the pain of rejection will be repeated; fear of death; fear of life. Fear dominates and rules our lives and the lives of the people around us. On one occasion I found myself talking to someone who, having moved away from the home she had lived in all her life, was desperate to return, for fear that if she did not, she would go mad. Fear has as its basis the threat of destruction – be it real or supposed. We know that within ourselves the fear of not being able to cope is rooted in the fear that our whole world will collapse around us. So our existence is spent shoring ourselves against the fears of that collapse.

Dealing with our own fear

Let us not bluff ourselves that we, as counsellors, are free from fear. It is as much part of our lives as it is part of those who come to us for help. So we too must come to grips with it, for if we do not, it is unlikely that we will be able to do much more than listen attentively to those who come to us. Jesus gives us at least two answers to the problems of fear. The first is to recognise that in the most fearful of situations we can and must expect that he is there and, being there, he is in control, no matter whether we feel it or not.

I come back repeatedly to the stilling of the storm and Jesus asleep in the boat. The anguished cries of the disciples, accusing and almost blaming him – "Do you not care that we perish?" – reflect our own sense of helplessness and panic as we face the unknown and realise that we are being swamped by forces that we cannot control or divert. Yet, in that situation, as the storm and our panic rise, Jesus *is* in control. This is the heart of the Gospel: that he is there, able to rebuke

the chaos around us and bring it under control, thereby giving
the peace which "passes understanding".

I have had only a limited experience of exorcism and
demon possession. What experience I have had has shown me
that in that situation fear emerges as a potent and almost
tangible force. I also know that, faced with that fear, it is at
the name of Jesus alone that the demons tremble and take
flight. I have seen and been involved with demoniacs and I
have been reminded of the storms of that sea and the absolute
stillness and quiet authority of our Lord in that situation. And
the quiet and peace after the demoniac has received release is
almost unbearable in its depth and sense of awe. The Holy
Spirit in that situation is a spirit of the peace of God, which
surpasses all human understanding.

The same sense of authority is seen at Jesus's trial. His
silence and controlled authority is in almost direct contrast to
the hysterical malevolence, or disdainful indifference of those
around him. I read recently of a person imprisoned and
tortured in one of the South American countries, who tes-
tified to the power of the Spirit in the face of overwhelming
fear, to bear witness to their interrogators and to communicate a calm and an authority which they did not feel. In fact,
many of the Christians in the prison believed that it was only
through their being interrogated that the interrogators themselves would hear the Gospel. So, in spite of their fear, their
torture and often their deaths, they believed implicitly in the
unalterable truth that even while chaos reigned, they were
able to know that Jesus is the Lord, even over the terrifying
chaos and evil in which they are immersed. This same experience has also been related to me by those suffering a similar
fate in this and other countries. All of this means that we must
be aware of our own fear and the need to come to grips with it
for ourselves.

Counselling in the face of fear

Fear takes a great number of forms and many of these will be dealt with in later chapters. Let me look at the aspects of fear, which will not be dealt with later.

Shame and panic

I have a vivid memory of dealing with a person who was so frightened of meeting new people, that he would do almost anything to avoid them. I was always fascinated that at the same time he entertained the idea of one day becoming a minister! It became clear that at some point in his fairly early life, his father had made fun of him in public and he had run out of the room with his family and some visitors laughing at him. The pain of this experience and the humiliation continued, in that every time there was company, his father did the same thing. Eventually the son would not come out of his room when there were guests. As he grew older, he made sure he was not even in the house if he knew there was to be company. Later, apart from the resentment he felt for his father, his own sense of worthlessness – of shame and humiliation – was such that whenever he met someone (bright and intelligent though he was) he simply could not bear to have any contact with them, in case they saw him as he "really" was, and he was shamed again. It got to the point when he would panic if it was even suggested that he meet someone new.

Helping him to a sense of his own worth (fear not little flock you are worth more . . .) was a long and at times tedious process. But the start of the self-acceptance came when I helped him, rather in the manner described by Ruth Carter Stapleton,[34] to have the courage to walk into the area of fear and relive the memory of that first humiliation. As he did, with all the emotions bubbling up in him, he saw also that, as he went out of the room, shamed and in tears, with laughter ringing in his ears, Jesus very gently took him by the hand, and they went out together. From that awareness of Jesus sharing his shame, and loving him when others laughed, came a healing which, while slow and often dispiriting, was nevertheless real. The aim of counselling in that situation was to

accept him as he was. As counsellor, I had to show a love for
him which he had never felt before, and that, too, was a test of
my patience and perseverance. Initially, I was aware, for
example, that a smile in the wrong place could easily have
meant a setback in our relationship, as he might well have
believed that I, too, was laughing at and rejecting him.

So fear and panic are overcome by faith – helping the
person to *trust* that, no matter what the circumstances, Jesus
the Lord of life and creation takes him seriously and loves him
deeply and calms the storms of chaos which threatens to
disintegrate him. In the process he will learn to start loving
himself and that is what Jesus wants, for self-love – self-
acceptance if you prefer – is what Jesus offers as the first step
to loving others. In the first Epistle of John, we are told,
"There is no fear in love, but perfect love casts out fear."[35]
This is a word of life if we can accept that "perfect love" is the
"I am" who makes himself known in Jesus and who comes to
us walking on the waters of chaos.

The truth will make you free

In counselling, we are faced repeatedly with people who want
to believe, who *want* to grow, who want to "walk tall", and
yet are afraid – of anything, and often everything. We all
know fear and we all know that we need a saviour, but we are
also sufficiently sinful that we do not want to admit our fears
or our dependence.

There is a terrible moment in William Golding's *Lord of the
Flies* when one of the boys who has not been drawn into the
ruling class (made up of choirboys!) on the island (the rulers
have used the fact of a mysterious presence at the top of the
hill to intimidate and control the other boys, though some
have not allowed themselves to be subject to those who are in
fact barbarians), goes up the hill to find out what in fact the
mysterious being is. Overcoming his terrror, he gets to the top
to discover that the "presence" is the flapping of the dead
pilot's parachute from the crashed plane which had brought
them to the island. Realising the truth, he rushes down to

spread the good news, only to be killed by the ruling class, because they prefer the truth to be concealed. If it is revealed for what it is, they will lose their control, for the fear will no longer be a working force.

The obvious allegorical similarity between this and the Gospels must be apparent. (Golding's book is a brilliant and frightening study in original sin and the forces of evil which it unleashes. The desire for power and control is so potent, that nice, "civilised" little boys become brutalising monsters and those who stand against them are often the odd men out – mocked or even physically unappealing, such as the short-sighted "Piggy". In the long run, they have to live a constant battle to withstand the fear engendered by their opponents and the devious schemes engineered to bring them under control.) What is also apparent, is that sin and evil are often the result of fear. The hardness of heart of the Pharisees and the radical rejection of Jesus by the Sadducees and the Herodians, are ample proof of that.

So, too, in our counselling we may well come across people who, if they are not themselves exploiting others' fears, are themselves being exploited. The selfish mother who manipulates the child to ensure that he or she stays at home; the 40-year-old spoilt only child (I have come across many such), who is little more than a puppet, are the victims of a deep fear that the parent will not be loved or cared for. (The fact that there is frequently no longer any love in the relationship is not apparently important.) That is a web of sin, and even when it is broken, the child has to learn new lessons as how to live without the prop – unless, as is sometimes the case, they have been dreaming of that for years!

Fear is therefore an instrument of sin, frequently used to distort the truth to its own advantage. Again, the counsellor may have very explicitly, though often very gently (sometimes not so gently), to show the other person the truth. The truth will always be in an area which apparently leaves another party disadvantaged – and therein lies the real fear. The counsellor may well have to act as a mediator and help the other party to a new set of values and insights. Again, Jesus can be the only answer. As he comes and shows us our own value and how we can stand and grow in new ways, we have the chance to know new truths in him, truths which will make us free, for they will not be distorted by fear.

So counselling in the areas of fear will involve helping people to face the fear and see it for what it is, a distortion which imprisons and gives neither peace nor hope. Fear makes it impossible to love adequately, or be loved. To face fear is to face the storms of chaos, or the abyss, to enter into those things we fear most and find Christ, alive and reigning.

Chapter
4

Anxiety

If fear is at the heart of sin and the human condition, it is anxiety closely related to fear as it is which permeates and forms a backdrop for much of our lives. Fear has a focus, anxiety has none, it is a state of worry in which a whole series of "maybe" or "perhaps" or "if only" pervade our attitudes, tying us down and frightening us by their very vagueness. Anxiety is as unspecific as fear is the opposite.

Fear in South Africa makes many white people assume that blacks are out to kill them and thus "all blacks are murderous" or at least potentially so. Fear makes blacks not trust the whites, so "no white is trustworthy"; the focus from both sides is specific and destructive. We may fear the bomb and many do for good reason; we may fear the politicians, who without any apparent morality other than what is right according to "the policy", appear happy to keep their finger close to the button to detonate the bomb. Fear is specific.

Anxiety is very much more vague. How will I cope? How will I have enough to eat? Will I be comfortable in my old age? Is my salary enough? What will people think of me? Will I be promoted if I say what I want or do what I ought? Anxiety tends to look to the future, and regard it with trepidation. Of course it *can* have a focus. The mother of the bride who has planned an outdoor reception or the rector of a parish whose bazaar is dependent upon the weather may both be justifiably anxious about the weather next week. The point is that neither can control the weather and the sense of dependence and the inability to control causes the anxiety which makes life very uncomfortable until the event is well under way.

Anxiety looks to the future, which cannot be controlled, and views all the possibilities of failure, of what others may do, of situations which may occur, and worries precisely because they cannot adequately be predicted, and as a result are outside one's area of authority. It is this sense of not being able to control events or situations which is at the heart of worry. So, if one is wanting some sort of definition of anxiety it is the inability of people to accept their creatureliness. There comes a point in life when, try as we may, or worry as we like (or dislike) we will not be able to change events or manipulate situations so as to take the danger out of them.

Victor Frankl (the "inventor" of the psychiatric insights associated with logotherapy) describes very movingly[1] how he came to that conclusion while interned in a Nazi concentration camp. As a Jewish intellectual he was singled out at times for "special" treatment, but in his acceptance of all that came his way he learned that life has a flow and a meaning which takes one beyond anxiety to the sort of confidence which made it possible to be creative and loving even in that hideous situation.

I have counselled innumerable people whose only problem is a vague and generalised worry, a feeling that all is not well, yet there is nothing specific or definable. The motivations of people to acquire more money, property, things, are often those of people who believe that if they can achieve enough of these things they will be secure. The problem is that having then achieved all their worldly goods, they worry about those too, in case they are removed. In that situation probably the only party which does not worry would be the insurance companies.

Underlying all of our worries is the fact of death; so once again, we are back with our creatureliness. We can try and put death off, we try somehow to sanitise it with euphemisms – passed on, crossed over – but death remains the greatest and most uncontrollable fact of life. It is no wonder that of all things we try to put death out of our consciousness; but it stays just beneath the surface, and there it affects our attitudes, our life, our relationships.

It is not surprising therefore that Jesus can help us to overcome fear, but he also is very realistic about anxiety. If anxiety does nothing else it creates a distortion of the truth, so that it is impossible to see things in their proper perspective. The truth is that God is the creator and Lord of history, and we mortals are creatures who have to accept our creatureliness and trust in a loving God who can and does use even the worst situation to his glory. The problem is that we are anxiously looking for *our* glory, and that is where things go wrong. So his teaching about anxiety and worry is straightforward and unequivocal. He assures us that as we see God preserving the tiniest elements of creation, so we, who are of much greater value than those elements, can confidently live our lives as disciples without fear. God's protective presence is on those who acknowledge him and look to him.[2] Thus if we put the authority of God first, and at the heart of life, then there will be no cause for worry, and there will be no cause for that all-pervading fear of death and meaninglessness.

More important, faith, the way we live so that God is really in the centre, is the only antidote to worry. It does not mean that all will be well, but that as we go through life, we have a purpose and a meaning which gives hope in situations otherwise pervaded by deep anxiety. Faith is at the heart of life lived without worry, so storing up earthly things is not going to help. The God who attends to the minutest details of creation is unlikely to abandon man, the high point of creation. Therefore, men need not worry – anxiety is for the unbelievers, the Gentiles, not for those who have been called to follow him. It is focused as always on the Kingdom of God. If we turn to the really important things – the reign of God – and work for that, then all the things which we worry about will be given as we need them.

The uncompromising part of Jesus's teaching, however, comes when he makes it clear that we must make a choice; it is impossible to give allegiance to two masters.[3] Having made the choice for the Kingdom, then there is no further need to worry. Luke takes it beyond even this point.[4] He, as with Matthew, assures the disciples that the Holy Spirit will guide them as to what they must say when they will be persecuted – so relax on that score![5] He reinforces the teaching about worry with the parable of the rich man who tried to store up all the wealth he needed, but had not faced the possibility of death.[6] And then, right at the end of this passage, prior to moving on to Jesus's teaching about preparedness to accept God when he comes, he tells his disciples, "fear not, little flock, for it is the Father's good pleasure to give you the Kingdom." If God is giving them the Kingdom, if God can trust them with *his* treasures, then they can, without concern, trust God, who is so much more trustworthy than they.

So it is back to faith, trust in a God who is Lord of history – and more involved in their unique lives than they are themselves. Faith alone removes the distortion and faith alone gives his followers the courage to move beyond their anxieties to a vision of creation which sees death as part of life and trust in God as a condition for life, and worries about nothing, for there is, in that context, no cause for worry.

The counsellor will come across a great deal of worry in his ministry. It is, as I have suggested, vague and unprecise, but very debilitating. The difficulty is to know how to handle it. There is no point in saying "Don't worry" because that solves nothing. It is also rather pointless to try to deal with it logically. A friend of mine has a physical condition which is both painful and disturbing. Medically it is not serious, but because the pain persists and he is seldom unaware of the condition, no amount of persuasion, argument, medical reassurance or clear logical thinking makes any difference. He is weighed down by the condition to the point where he is almost incapable of thinking of anything else. He believes in God and in many ways he trusts him, but he cannot move away from the anxiety created by the condition. I find that situation very difficult. I want to say to him something like this: "Surely it is better to accept the medical evidence and live a full and joyful life, taking the risk of the doctors being wrong, than to live a half life of worry." But the problem is that I cannot feel the way he does, so mine is a purely theoretical response, and is at its best only loving advice; on average the counsellor's advice should always be sparse and very much related to certainties. My ultimate hope with that person is to help him to come to terms with the worst: what if I do die? What if I am bed-ridden? What if I cannot work? Has not our Lord shown us that there is more to life than these things? If he has led us to this point, will he not lead us beyond it to a life fuller and richer than one filled with anxiety about a condition which I cannot cure and a death I cannot avoid? For so many of us the thought of death is a final defeat, yet Jesus has shown us that it is a present reality and a part of the purpose of life. So faith, the trust that God is in fact in control, that he loves and cares for us uniquely, is the only way past the immediate problems. But more is necessary. Again it is a question of perspectives. What do we achieve by worrying? That is the question Jesus puts to us. The answer lies in our ability to look past the immediate to the actual purpose of living. For the Christian, that purpose is to reflect the presence of the Lord who gives us life. That means that anxiety, all-pervading as it may be, must give way to what it means to "seek first the Kingdom of God". The priority of life is always to reflect the obedience to which he calls us and live joyfully, in the sure knowledge that come what may, God's authority will finally triumph. There is no need to bolster our insecurity, or hedge ourselves around with false securities. We *can* live freely and we *are* his children whom he has promised not to forsake. So the purpose of life takes us to a vision for the world and for ourselves which must always keep our eyes on God's authority as we know it in Jesus, and experience it in the Spirit.

And what of the counsellor's anxieties? Again, we must be sure that we do not bluff ourselves. We too have to face the unspecific threats, the ominous fact of death, our own faith-lessness and our terrible insecurities. For me there are no easy answers. I know the vision of the joyful obedient life and I have staggered towards that vision often enough, only to slip back into feelings of anxiety which negate so much of what I teach and stand for. The sea of worry on which I float with dreadful self-importance is no place to drown. And the only answer is to look up and see Jesus, to hear him ask me where my faith is, or whether I have grown any as a result of all my worry. In that situation we are called upon to trust. Trusting is easy when all goes well, but to be faithful when life is full of worry is very difficult. Yet it is the only way to once more catch a glimpse of the Lord who looked worry in the face and trusted in the will of the Father. That trust led him through anxiety to the new life which he offers us in exchange for our anxieties.

Chapter
5

Anger

We cannot escape anger. In my country anger is so much part
of life that we almost take it for granted. Violence, which is
one expression of anger, is not unique to South Africa, it boils
up easily and erupts often when we least expect it. A friend of
mine who was rector of a parish in which there were some
devastating riots several years ago, said, "A mob is a mindless
thing." That sums up anger in its violent state. It is an
emotional condition so strong that it does a brain bypass
and so the actions and reactions are raw, destructive and
tragic.

The riots in South Africa which have exploded from time to
time, or those in the United States in the late 1960s and early
1970s, or the wars of "liberation", or whatever, are all fuelled
by anger, exploitation, a feeling of frustration – and fear. I
believe the same could be said of the more recent riots in
Brixton and Toxteth. Unemployment, discrimination and
frustration explode into the angry violence of people who
know no other way of expressing themselves. And here too
fear is at the heart of the angry response. So we are back to
that again – we can scarcely go anywhere without fear reap-
pearing.

Anger is the source of so much of what we feel and do, and,
while it may be irrational and "mindless", it is nevertheless
the chief response to our greatest fear – rejection. To be
treated as a nobody is the worst insult of all and what we all
tend to fear the most because there is in most of us a deep
feeling that we are nobodies anyway. To have that confirmed
is to be forced to take the possibility seriously and in that

situation our anger boils to the surface, to erupt in violence, whether of deed or word, or both. Our feelings of rejection are so strong that our angers will try to destroy anything which somehow confirms that rejection.

So blacks will want to destroy the whites, who are holding them back – and down; whites will want to destroy those who, by their very numbers, different cultures and pigmentation, pose a threat to the comfort and values in which they have invested so much of themselves. Those who seek to effect reconciliation are regarded as traitors or sellouts, in both camps. It is an uncomfortable place in which to be!

Anger can therefore lead to violence – that is anger when it "blows outwards". There is another form of anger which turns inwards; it is not expressed, often not even known in any overt way, but is, in its way, just as potent. It leads to depression, which has been called "frozen anger", anger on ice, but that ice is very close to boiling if given half a chance.

So again in South Africa we have many people who, because they cannot express their anger, or have release from the causes of their anger, are depressed, individually and as a society. We have one of the highest suicide rates in the world, I am told, and that includes blacks and whites; we have people whose daily hope of gaining any self-esteem is the possibility of being approved of by those in authority; outside that situation they have no hope, no future and no possibility of rising to any level of self-acceptance. Self-acceptance through acceptance by others is so often what we seek. If we can please others we are happy and feel loved. But love in that context becomes a fawning, self-congratulatory thing, where we sell ourselves to any who may remotely appreciate us, in the hope that we may find what is in practice a spurious acceptance. Look at any business enterprise and see the same thing. Look at that same enterprise and see people clawing for promotion, so that they may know they have some worth; sunk in gloom if it does not come, looking, working for a few words of praise to raise the soul and alleviate the terrible feeling of being a nobody which haunts us continually.

No one can avoid anger, it is as much part of us as the air we breathe, yet many people, because they feel that they cannot or ought not express it, suppress it – with disastrous consequences, for that leads only too frequently to depression. Of course, depression does not usually look like anger. It manifests itself as self-indulgent, self-pitying with no hope and no vision. At its worst, it is paralysing and creates the sort of situation where the person cannot work, cannot relate, cannot sleep, and cannot even feel. It is as though there is a dam waiting to burst inside us and the wall may be well made and have the strength to keep back the forces of anger and fear. More often than not, the wall will *feel* safe while we live a life which we have made for ourselves, so that rejection is kept at a convenient distance and acceptance is comfortably close, be it at work or with family and friends. The crisis comes when situations change – a loved one dies; we are promoted and are afraid we cannot really do the job; we change jobs; a man packs up everything and starts training for the ministry; we move home to another place where we are strangers in a strange land.

Another cause of crisis may well come in a very different, but no less important way. A person may come to a new experience of God, which will give him a tremendous sense of freedom, joy and love. He will also, perhaps surprisingly, become aware of areas of fear, temptation and anger in himself, which he did not know existed. Very frequently, if he tries to express these "bad" feelings to others with whom he is involved, for example his prayer group, he will be told that those are not the sort of things which Christians should feel. This will only make the feelings worse, because they cannot be expressed – not, at least, to the people who have accepted him most and loved him deeply prior to his expressing his feelings. That too will feel very like rejection.

The list is endless: the carefully constructed world of acceptance disintegrates, the dam wall breaks, but we dare not let the angers out, even if we feel them as angers. They are probably more likely to be felt as fears, incompetence, rejection, strangeness, but the angers are there, burning inwardly and burning the sap from our life, leaving us lethargic, tired and very, very sorry for ourselves, often without even knowing why. The counsellor will see all this quickly and know that the fires of rage are burning. It is for him to help the person to face those fires, not being afraid of them or ashamed either. He is to help that person locate the areas of his anger and bring him into an awareness of what it means for his rage and the attendant feelings to be absorbed by our loving God.

Jesus's teaching about anger

We have seen, at least briefly, in an earlier chapter, how Jesus dealt with his own anger – anger at seeing the things of God and, indeed, the presence of God, trampled in the market place or denied for fear that they might be true. Now let us look at what Jesus has to say about anger in other people's lives.

The obvious place to begin is the Sermon on the Mount.[1] Here Jesus's teaching up-ends that which has been taken for granted by the Jews in their law. Starting with the Beatitudes,[2] he reverses so many of the values which we assume are right. So a gentleness, a forgiving and loving nature enters our relationships as we listen to him. He directs us to a different type of attitude, where meekness, righteousness, mercy, poverty of Spirit, pureness of heart, peace and even submission are signs of *loving the other person rather than crying for one's rights.* So much of Jesus's teaching actually focuses us away from ourselves, to accept the other person as he is and, in the process, to overwhelm him with love – the last thing he would expect or think he wants. This attitude will lead to persecution, but it is the sort of persecution which will wear the persecutor down by the love which is directed at him.[3] It is also more easily said than done;

one of the important things about the Sermon on the Mount is that it requires a commitment to the preacher, before it makes any real sense to the listener. That commitment is to him as Messiah, and his teaching is the new Law, given to the true Israel of God, that we may live out the reality of God's presence in our lives. So, when he comes to deal with anger, we expect that he will turn that upside down too, which is what he does.

Essentially, Jesus says[4] that murder is an act which can be seen and recognised for what it is. But what of your motives: your desires; your attitudes of revenge and insult? Those are things which cannot be measured and yet they are as destructive *of you* as the desire to kill or the act of killing is, of the person killed. So, if you feel like that, then, while you have time, go and lovingly make it up with the person with whom you are angry, if for no other reason, than that he might himself get back at you.

Essentially, that is true of any who have anything against you; a loving concern for the other person dissipates the anger and gives a new value to the relationship. As we have already seen, that is his basic teaching about anxiety, only then he calls for a loving trust in God as the all-caring and providing Father. The point to notice is an obvious one: he does not tell us not to be angry, but he does say that if anger leads to sinful desires, then he gives us ways to deal with the anger, which turns the power of that attitude into something creative and loving.

Anger makes us boss-eyed – when angry we can see neither straight nor clearly. Jesus recognised that too and there are several incidents where he dealt with anger by simply pointing out the truth, rather than by allowing it to continue into an even more destructive rage. So we see him, in John's Gospel, caught in controversy with the Jews.[5] Essentially, they try to discredit his work by suggesting that he cannot be authentic, because he did not go to a duly accredited theological seminary![6] That does not work and Jesus turns the decision to an understanding of God's glory. If you keep the law by circumcising on the Sabbath, ought not I to keep the law by making a man whole on the Sabbath? And, in that context, he asks them why they should be angry at him for effectively keeping the Sabbath so much more fully. The anger described here is not the burning anger mentioned in Matthew's Gospel, but the sour-tasting feeling of resentment and antagonism which gives a real sense of calculated viciousness, as opposed to something more passionate. Thus, anger here is the more sinful, because it consumes like a cancer of the gall bladder, rather than the fires which burn in the belly. They are both destructive and sinful, but they are dealt with in different ways. Of course, the cold anger can burst into flames when sparked.

The parable[7] of the prodigal son[8] seems to give us some awareness of that. Reading into the parable at least a little, we have a picture of the elder son, whose self-righteousness is at least partly built on his suppressed anger at his younger brother's behaviour and attitudes. He, who has served his father so well, feels excluded and taken for granted – causes of anger in many of us. The sight of the rejoicing over the return of the despised brother sets off his deep-seated anger – so great, that he excludes himself from the festivities. Again, Jesus's answer to that sort of anger, given to us in the form of the father's answer in the parable, is to put the thing in perspective and to show that, far from the father rejecting him, he is as much beloved as the younger son, which in no way nullifies the joy he feels at the son's return.

We shall look elsewhere at what I have called the Prodigal Son Syndrome in counselling – the desire for people to go off on their own and "do their own thing", and for the counsellor to let them, or to help others to let them. Now, we simply note that the angers reflected in the parable are also dealt with by means of an absorbent love and the pointing out of the truth, which is the only thing which can start the process towards resolution of the anger, a resolution which begins with an assurance of love. The need to accept that love is still a necessity for the one who feels the anger.

Jesus in the face of anger

I am going to focus this section specifically on the Cross, for in that setting alone do we see Jesus's full answer to the problems of anger. I will not hesitate to move from one Gospel to the other, as we deal with the events of the Passion, though I am always conscious that, even here, the Gospel writers are interpreting the events somewhat differently, to try to say different things about God's action and our salvation.

The anger which Jesus has to face is of the cold, calculated variety; as well as the violent, unthinking kind of the mob. As we understand the Gospels, the plotting to kill Jesus starts early, as he forces the kingdom of evil on to the defensive. So, in Mark, the beginning of Chapter 3 sees the religious and secular authorities in a conspiracy, culminating in carefully made plans, aided and brought to fruition by the treachery of Judas.[9] Later, before Caiaphas,[10] we see Jesus in what feels and looks like a kangaroo court, as they try desperately to make a charge stick. It is only when he says "I am",[11] when they ask whether he is the Christ (thus again using the divine name), that their anger, which until this point has been cold and hard, even if somewhat desperate, explodes into a fury as their worst suspicions are confirmed. He is a blasphemer – for it is beyond their sight to accept him as Messiah. So Jesus is beaten up, spat upon and abused. All of which he accepts and absorbs in silence. The truth was more than they could stand.

In the trial before Pilate[12] he is the victim, not only of the anger of the Jews and the indifference of Pilate, but also of mob violence, as they bay for blood – his blood. The irony of Barabbas's release is heightened by the "envy" of the Jewish rulers and the desire of the crowd to have Barabbas released. That it was a put-up job is unimportant to the crowd – "we want him and we'll get him" seems to be their attitude. So Jesus dies at the hands of Roman executioners, a terrible and agonised death. Yet, even here, as the nails pound into his arms and feet, he is able to absorb the anger: "Father forgive them, for they know not what they do."[13]

His ordeal is not over, however. Strung out on the Cross, abused and still the target of anger and derision, his words are all loving. Care for his mother,[14] care for the penitent thief,[15] and, indeed, for the impenitent one, his own sense of Godforsakenness,[16] the commitment of himself to the Father,[17] the thunderous declaration in John, "It has been accomplished" (It is finished),[18] are all expressions of his loving involvement with people, whose hatred and anger want only to see him destroyed. It is this preparedness to let them; his acceptance of them, *even as they are rejecting him*, that is his answer to anger. It is the loving silence, the word spoken at the right time, the living out of what it means in the Sermon on the Mount to "bless them who persecute you". There is no greater power on earth and it is not surprising that Paul, meditating as he does, so effectively, on the Cross, is able to say, "Do not be overcome by evil, but overcome evil with good."[19]

What does this say for our counselling?

As I have been writing these past few pages, I have been listening to the unbelievable power of Beethoven's Fifth Symphony. It has always seemed to me that it starts, not with Fate knocking at the door, but with anger at the inevitable deafness creeping up on him. That theme continues throughout the symphony, but it ends, as I hear it, with a glorious acceptance of his lot and a realisation that what seems an awful destiny may itself prove to be the opening to even greater music. The rest of his symphonies seem to show that that was true. Essentially it seems that we must surely regard anger in the same way. It is sinful when it is used viciously and destructively; it is sinful when it gives rise to desires for vengeance or suicide, but we cannot escape it in ourselves, nor can we expect others not to feel it. It is, as I say, a primary response to rejection and how it expresses itself is, as we have seen, dependent on the personality and reactions of the person concerned. The counsellor usually comes across anger, in whatever form, when the person cannot cope. Mostly people *can* cope but, as I suggested at the beginning of this chapter, it is often when a crisis occurs in their life that they need help.

Most people are not aware of the dark foreboding angers which may well go back to their time in the womb. They know they get depressed, or that they lose their temper, but they are unaware of the forces which produce those feelings. When the feelings become "more than I can cope with", they may well turn to someone for help. Initially, they will feel better simply talking about it and the release of that pressure is a great relief. It is thus critical that the counsellor is prepared to spend time helping him look, not at his immediate relationships, but at his primary ones: parents, brothers and sisters.

I once had to deal with a deeply depressed person on an extended basis. It became clear that, though he could not cope then, in fact he had never really been able to cope. He hated his father and his grandfather, he could not believe that his wife loved him; his mother had died when she should not have – he felt she had let him down – his grandmother was no substitute. It was as we looked at these relationships, looking carefully at them – "Did your father actually mock you, or was it his way of expressing love?" – that two things became clear: his anger had made him unable to see properly; and he had in fact not known the truth. Yet he had acted on the untruth with all the feelings of rejection and anger and these had stayed with him all his life and, like an avalanche, had gathered evidence with every relationship. On their honeymoon he and his wife had been golfing. He had not been very skilful at the game and at one shot, had missed the ball completely. She had laughed; he had interpreted that as rejection. Years later they were able to talk of that incident and she was able to point out the truth of the incident: it was a loving laugh, not a mocking one.

And so it went; hours of the same sort of thing. And all the time, I found myself filled with an overwhelming sense of love for him, which I tried to communicate by not laughing and not passing off what might have seemed trivial as of no consequence. The angers which he felt were *gradually* replaced with a self-acceptance and a love of many people who had threatened him in their relationships.

On another occasion I was counselling a young woman who had a terrible anger against her mother. Having reached a point of real love for the mother I suggested that the young woman write a letter of apology for the deliberate hurt she had inflicted, and also expressing the love which she now felt. The letter was itself one of the most moving I have ever seen and the response of the mother was overwhelmingly loving and grateful. It opened the door to a new relationship between them.

Yes, anger often needs to find an expression as part of the recovery, in penitence, to God, of course, but also to those who have been hurt and maligned in the process. It needs to be helped to die down so that the fires which burn so aggressively, even when hidden, may no longer affect each relationship in a perverse way. The counsellor must himself meditate on what it means to "abide" in Christ; to rest peaceably in the loving presence of a living Saviour, and he needs to help others to do the same. Of all the counselling I have done, anger in all its forms requires that sense of the gentle presence of God most of all. In union with the loving, accepting source of life, angers die and love – bold, decisive and powerful – rises in its place.

When I gave this chapter to a friend of mine to look at in its original form, his reaction was: "It is all very well to talk about absorbing anger and giving out love, but that places a terrible burden on me, because I am sure I cannot do that." My response to what I consider a valid response, is: "That is the way Jesus did it." He absorbed the anger of mankind and loved them to death. That is not the only way. There are many times as we have seen that Jesus dealt with anger and hardness of heart by pointing to the truth; by getting things in proportion; by meeting anger with a like and powerful emotion, sometimes anger, usually grief or compassion.

The counsellor will recognise that most of the anger with which he deals will be an expression of rejection in some form or another. It may well be justified. Exploitation, patronisation and oppression, in whatever form, is legitimate cause for anger. The problem is how to deal with the anger so that it is creative. On the personal level, the best way is to talk to the other person, long before the angers have reached flash point. That may not always be possible. Then the counsellor will have to be the talking block; he will have to help keep the anger in proportion and at the same time help the person to a plan of action which will be creative. If we do that, then angers will burn for the righteousness of God; the angers of others will be absorbed in a loving concern for them; the frustrations and indignities to which we are so easily subject will be the weapons whereby love may be expressed, anger directed creatively and "the world" overcome.

Depression

I have mentioned depression throughout this chapter, now let us have a look at some elements of counselling the depressed person. I am convinced that with one possible exception, every depressed person with which I have had anything to do has become depressed because of an anger somewhere in their lives. That anger, or its cause, may not readily be seen, but I have yet to come across the situation when it is not there. The onset of depression is fascinating, for it seems to come unexpectedly. The post-natal depression of the mother whose child ties her down or makes such demands that she feels she cannot cope. The anger there is directed at the baby, or the husband, but it is difficult to express, so it turns inward. The new Christian who wants to do things right and has been taught to believe in absolutes – absolute commitment, complete love, total involvement – only to discover that sin and self negate them. The anger and fear of hell judgment focus on others who either push them into the unobtainable absolutes, or who do not seem to live up to them; frequently those angers turn into self-accusation and the depression is very severe.

More often the depression is in response to a feeling of not being able to cope in a context where we feel overwhelmed. The angers created by one's own inabilities turn inwards because there is nothing on which they can be vented. Then the depression descends like a blanket, enveloping and suffocating any creative response. Depression causes an inability to work, react, play, laugh or even cry. At its worst it is a psychotic condition, which needs hospitalisation and medical care. More often it is a see-saw thing; down one day and right the next, depending on circumstances.

The need is not so much to find the anger, though that may be possible, as to understand what it means to "abide" in the Lord, in the way described by John's Gospel. To find one's being in a God who is not so much activist as loving, and to learn to love God and accept his will. This will mean learning to be still, to relax physically and let go emotionally, to let the fires of anger turn to fires of love. It will mean once again getting things in perspective and accepting that God is not calling us to cope in our strength so much as to be obedient in his. It is the loving obedience to a God who does give us the ability to cope as we are ourselves given the ability to abide in him.

Chapter
6

Self-acceptance

As a schoolboy I was brought up to believe that to love oneself was the height of self-centredness. To say to another that he loved himself was a terrible insult, implying arrogance sufficiently unpleasant as to create the possibility of avoiding him altogether. It came then as a considerable surprise – indeed, a considerable shock – to have a wise and loving priest friend of mine tell me that I did not love myself. He said it not as a congratulation, but in a worried way, as one who was concerned for my spiritual well-being. Having grown up *not* to love myself, I could not *really* understand what he was saying and even today I find that, while I can tell myself intellectually that it is right for me to love myself, emotionally it is a much tougher battle; at times I think it may be a losing one. As I have been helped to look back over particular areas of my life (with which I am not going to regale you), I can understand why I had felt unloveable and in that knowledge have been able to move more confidently into an attitude of self-acceptance.

The context in which the priest friend told me I did not love myself was a conference where, for a number of reasons, I had taken quite a battering. Bruised (emotionally) and *very* sore and sorry for myself, I turned to him and he sat and talked to me for several hours until eventually, exhausted and unhappy, I went to bed well after 2 a.m. The conference called for an early start – 6.30 Eucharist – so it was with a sense of astonishment and joy that I woke at 5.45 to find my friend, clothed, washed and shaved, sitting on my bed and enquiring with a concern I had never experienced or believed possible whether I was all right. It occurred to me then that whatever I thought of myself, at least one other person thought I was worth putting himself out for. That was a shock too. The words were something, but the actions spoke so much more clearly – and are wonderfully fulfilling. That dear friend of mine is dead now but he started me on a path which has led to my being able to love others better and love myself more fully.

It is only when I *accept* that God loves me, that I am a son of God, that I am united with him in Our Lord Jesus and bonded into the fellowship of the Holy Spirit, the Church, that I *dare* to love others, dare to be humble and joyful, and dare to accept the hardships and difficulties which following Christ must inevitably bring. Roger Hurding[1] has a marvellously simple diagram which shows that self-acceptance is the core of our ability to love God as well as to love others. He also has another diagram, which shows the opposite approach when we are caught in self-rejection.

Many times in the course of counselling, I have asked people, quite urgently at times, whether they love themselves? Almost without exception, the answer is "of course not" and usually, if they are Christian, it is followed by a remark such as "that is sinful". The point is that true self-love is *not* sinful, it is the beginning of knowing oneself as a complete and, wonder of wonders, loveable person. Because we do not love ourselves, we embark upon a whole host of false trails. Some of them have been mentioned already – the people whose self-image, and therefore self-acceptance, is dependent on the approval of others: boss, friends, spouse, *anybody*, just as long as the word of approval is there. It is a false trail, because no one can achieve at that rate all the time and anything less than congratulatory or approving is regarded as rejection, which secretly confirms our own unloveableness. John describes the attitude well, when he says of the authorities that "They loved the praise of men more than the praise of God."[2]

There are other false trails as well. Success, in terms of

position and money, status in society, popularity and the desire to be first with the latest. Is not gossip and the need to be on the inside with all the confidences, part of a process of building up a self-acceptance, which is constantly in danger of disintegrating? The world of politics is full of people who want to be on the inside, so that they can "be" someone; and politics, it must be remembered, is not limited to governments. Universities, the Church, businesses, big and small, are all riven with political intrigues which frequently have at their core people who are seeking to cover their own feelings of inadequacy and rejection, by building something which will prove to themselves and hopefully to others that they are in fact of value after all. It is not surprising, therefore, that Jesus had some important things to say about self-acceptance.

Jesus's teaching on self-acceptance

We have seen in an earlier chapter that Jesus had to come to terms with himself as an integral part of his ministry to others. Thus, the awareness of himself in relation to "Abba" lies at the basis of his self-knowledge and acceptance and this emerges in his ability to speak with authority, to declare a new Law ("but I say to you") and most powerfully in the "I am" sayings in John's Gospel. The wonder of Jesus's self-acceptance is that he gives us the opportunity to accept ourselves as well. We start with a strange little saying: "For what does it profit a man, to gain the whole world and forfeit his life?"[3] The context of this passage is persecution. If the disciples are to follow Jesus and acknowledge him as Messiah, then they are to accept the cost of that acknowledgement – for it will be in conflict with many others who claim total allegiance. To deny Jesus in that context carries with it the hope of staying alive and accepting the approval of those with counter claims, most notably the Roman Empire, but the cost is too great, for in the process he will "forfeit his life", he will be one of the walking dead. He will have cut himself off from the very source of life. Thus, at the heart of discipleship is the denial of the things which the world takes for granted – security and stability as the world sees them – in order to achieve another kind of stability and security in the age to come. Yet, while that is still true in many contexts today, and many followers of our Lord throughout the world are called upon to make that agonised choice in political and persecution situations, it is also true in less dramatic ways. It is against the background of Jesus's own acceptance of his status as Messiah on *his* terms, that we see the possibilities of self-acceptance. It is because he is not prepared to take with the title "Messiah", as declared by Peter only a short while before,[4] all the trappings of current Jewish expectations that he begins to teach them that "the Son of Man (the title he seems to use most of himself) *must* suffer many things". So his own identity is linked with his suffering; and the identity of his disciples is in their preparedness to follow wherever he leads them.

Those who would follow Jesus must accept the possibility of being stripped of all that seems really important: status, class, educational achievements, to say nothing of popularity and the voices which, while calling for compromise, offer new life, salvation and security if only their adherents will follow blindly. Those voices are the most insidious of all because, as is the case with most governments, the salvation and security is thought to be most effective when it is hedged by armaments and arsenals of power.

Jesus gives us a new identity. As his disciples, we are offered a perspective which goes beyond physical security to true identity – in him; and the possibility of *self-acceptance based on nothing other than allegiance to Him*. The strange thing is that self-acceptance is based on the rather contradictory thought that to attain one's life, one has to lose it, and the more one tries to gain, the less one actually achieves. To turn outwards is to grow inwards; to put oneself where Jesus is, is to achieve what we so badly want: self-acceptance; the completeness which comes from him alone. That may be hard, but then at no point did Jesus say it would be easy. Easiness, when it *is* mentioned as part of discipleship, is related to his "yoke", and that sounds very much like being under a fairly rigorous discipline. It is the acceptance of his yoke which is the clue to that little saying,[5] for it is that "acceptance" which makes the yoke "easy". When we turn to the obvious passage on self-acceptance, we have interesting things here too.[6] The context in each case is controversy with the men learned in the Law and, in each case, they are seeking to show that he who has set himself up as an authority is not in fact as good as he thinks. The point for us is that the Law is quoted in terms of the Shema – the embodiment of Judaism in these two sayings. What Jesus does is give new content to them. The fact is that the Book of Leviticus tells us to love others as we love ourselves,[7] and Jesus approves of the Scribes' answer. It focuses in three directions – God, others, ourselves. All three objects of our love are necessary if we are going to be whole people. It is very difficult to love ourselves in isolation, which is what Jesus was trying to communicate in the passage on forfeiting one's life.

Loving oneself is thus taken for granted, but what is meant by it? The Greek word for "love" is almost impossible to translate; it is too rich and full for one overworked word like "love". It means so much more than liking, or even "object of affection". It has a sense of self-giving and self-denying – which takes us back to the previous passage. Jesus is saying something like this: "Give of yourself as wholeheartedly to others as you do to your own needs and interests, do not hold back or hesitate in that giving, for it is essentially you." It stands to reason then, that if I cannot give myself wholeheartedly to my own needs and interests, or if I am so obsessed by them that I cannot see that others have them too, then I am unlikely to be very loving either to others or God or myself. For then love of self becomes self-indulgence, and love of others is reduced to currying favour in the hope that others may respond. And love of God then becomes no more than a grasping after a false security, for it is not love which one is after, but cosseting or protection.

So when Jesus approves of the summary of the Law, which tells us to love our neighbour as ourself, he is reinforcing what he says elsewhere, when he tells us "as you wish that men would do to you, do so to them". Then he forces the point home by showing that love does not involve just loving the people with whom you are most comfortable – there is no self loss there, "for even sinners lend to sinners to receive as much again". Rather, he says, "Love your enemies and do good and lend, expecting nothing in return and your reward will be great and you will be *sons of the Most High*."[8] Jesus is quite clear that people, all people, have a value which they must accept and enjoy. It is the acceptance of that value which makes it possible for them to stand in the sure knowledge of who they are and, in the process, take whatever the world throws at them. I have heard it said that the people who do not break under torture are those who have such a sense of their own value and identity that nothing "the world" can do is able to break it. That, too, is the impression given by Polycarp, who when asked to reject Jesus says quite simply: "eighty-six years have I served Him, and He has done me no wrong: how then can I blaspheme my King who saved me."[9] Stephen, too, at his death, is able to stand and see the glory of God and, at the moment of his death, turn and ask forgiveness for those stoning him.[10]

Jesus's teaching on human value comes in various places. He says we are of more value than the birds[11] and the flowers;[12] he makes it clear that God takes infinite pains to find those who are lost.[13] The point is that penitence is essential, for it implies a desire to return to God. So again we come back to what it means to deny oneself and take up one's cross. If Jesus makes it clear that we have *more value* than any other part of creation, he also makes it clear that we cannot achieve any semblance of self acceptance without him. He declares that he has come to the lost sheep of Israel,[14] even though the Canaanite woman's daughter is healed as a result of her mother's faith; he also affirms that he is the physician who heals the sick. Those who think they have "arrived", who are well, have no need of a physician.[15] The same element is communicated in the parable of the Pharisee and the sinner.[16] The man who is justified in the parable is the one who knows that he is dependent on God and, in his humility, is able to deny himself the righteousness which the Pharisee sees as so important.

Jesus helping others to self-acceptance

One of the delightful incidents in the Gospels is that involving the rather odious little man Zacchaeus and Jesus.[17] One cannot help thinking of Zacchaeus as the sort of person who, because of his size, has always been pushed around. That may or may not be true, but what is clear is that he has turned traitor to his own people, has acted as an agent for the Romans, and has amassed considerable wealth. It seems that Zacchaeus is nevertheless fascinated by Jesus. Perhaps he had heard that this man Jesus at least talked to the likes of him, which is more than anyone else did. So his climbing into the tree represents a possibly forlorn attempt to see someone who has the sort of love which he himself has long since lost; if he ever had it. The mere presence of Jesus in his house is enough to bring Zacchaeus to a state of new life or, as Jesus says, salvation. It starts with penitence – it ends with self-acceptance. In the process, there is reparation for sin recognised. The self-acceptance is seen quite clearly in relation to Jesus's acceptance of him and his new-found status as a "son of Abraham". Here, indeed, is Jesus coming to a lost sheep of the house of Israel. Several things must be noticed in this incident:

Jesus looked up and saw him. The initiative belongs to Jesus and he uses it to see him, not as a sinner, a tax collector, a wealthy man, a midget (or very nearly one), or even a rather strange, perhaps not very nice, little man in a tree. Jesus sees *him*, a human being, unloved, unloving, bruised and hurt by the circumstances of life, unsuited to his wealth. Certainly Zacchaeus was unacceptable to those around him, and very much, one would imagine, unacceptable to himself. Yet Jesus saw him as an object of love and acceptance.

Jesus's presence in his house is enough to give to Zacchaeus new life and a new purpose for living; a desire to make reparation, and a desire to make a new start. It is only as *Zacchaeus denied himself*, that he was able to come to an acceptance of his new status as a son of Abraham. What a wonderful possibility that a man, who is so rejected by others and himself, may find a new status within himself and with those around him, simply because Jesus moved into his house briefly for a meal.

What was true of Zacchaeus was true also, it would appear, of the other tax collectors as well as the prostitutes of his day. They, according to Jesus, because they were aware of their need, were more acceptable, and thus "go into the Kingdom of God before you". While the religious authorities could not even accept John the Baptist, the scum of society were able to "believe him". The religiously acceptable, who ought to have been able to respond readily, were not able to "repent and believe him".[18]

Very frequently in Jesus's ministry, it is those unacceptable in society and, by their very activities unacceptable to themselves, who come to Him and find new life and identity as they accept Him as Saviour. Probably the most obvious case is that of Matthew, or Levi the son of Alphaeus, the tax collector, who abandoned all to follow Jesus.[19] In Mark's Gospel, this piece of information is followed by the criticism from the religious authorities, who disapproved of his involvement with the "tax collectors and sinners". The implication is clear: if one associates with that sort of person, then it is likely that one will be contaminated. The result is a rejection of his claims as Messiah; no one who mixes in that company can be Messiah. Jesus's response is uncompromising. If you do not think you are sinful enough to ask for and receive salvation, that is fine: "I came not to call the righteous, but the sinners."[20]

So we can see that the way Jesus deals with people as they

come to acceptance of themselves is entirely consistent with his teaching. He gives them a new vision of themselves, their own sin, and their own worth when the sin is drawn away. He shows them who they are and he loves them, in spite of the fact that they are unlovely. The transformation is miraculous. The same is possible with those who come to us for counselling.

The implications of this for counselling

There is a passage in St Paul which has always fascinated me and increasingly in counselling, I have found myself using it or adapting it to suit the situation. I am quoting from the NEB, which seems to give a fuller idea of what St Paul was trying to say: "Agree together my friends to follow my example. You have us for a model; watch those whose way of life conforms to it."[21] In two other places in his letters to the Corinthian Church, he exhorts them to "be imitators of me"[22] and, on a number of occasions, Paul makes it clear that the presence of God is visible in him.[23] Paul has no hesitation in saying that, as he has been subjected by the Spirit of God to conform to God's will and pattern in Christ Jesus, so the presence of Christ shines through him, for the benefit and salvation of those to whom he has been sent. He claims nothing for himself, other than a desire to be obedient to the Lord Jesus and the marks on his body prove his commitment. In fact, he makes it clear that all his hard-earned achievements in Judaism and his proud pedigree are so much garbage, compared to being stripped bare of all that and being subjected to the wonderful presence of Christ Jesus.[24]

The point is this: there are many times in counselling when the counsellor has to help a person by allowing the person to see Christ in him. The quality of our love, the ability to relate, the depth of our compassion, the involvement of our listening, will say a great deal in this regard. But there will be times when, like Paul, we will have to personify Christ to the person seeking counselling. That is not blasphemous; it means taking

seriously what it means for the Church to be the Body of
Christ. As a limb of that Body, we will represent Christ in that
specific situation. We will expect to be the presence of Christ
to that person – for how else will he know Christ, unless he
sees Him in us? There have been many times when I have
found it necessary to say to the person seeking counselling, "I
know that at this point it is difficult for you to trust God, or
even to experience his love, for he is not specially real to you.
For the moment, trust me, and accept my love and acceptance
of you. That is the first step in the process of knowing the
overwhelming love of God because at this moment, I am
representing God to you."

It is an awesome responsibility, but it is also a tremendous
privilege. As the person is aware that you accept him, even as
his sin emerges, as the ugliness (at least to him) of himself
starts to appear, so it is possible for the counsellor to love him
more and more, because one is loving the real person and not
an artificial, though fairly solid, smokescreen. As he becomes
aware of that love (and for a while he will be so bothered and
distressed by the feeling of being stripped naked, so that the
things in his life, which he has not dared look at, are exposed
to his gaze as well as that of someone else), he will be able to
accept your love and acceptance and then transfer it to where
it really belongs – God.

The counsellor has no need to fear the process, unless he
relies on his own skills and strength. He too knows that he is a
naked beggar, who is the object of the love of God. He too
knows that he is lovable, not because of any skills or worth
which he has built up, but because, while yet a sinner, Christ
died for him. So he goes into the process of counselling with
many skills, all of them given by God, and no security other
than that Christ has called him into this relationship and that
he is no more than a servant doing his job. The glory is that he
is Christ's servant, and that is all that really matters.

The person seeking help is also to be exposed to the loving
acceptance of God in other ways. He will know it in the
counsellor, he will experience it in the counsellor's patience

and persistence, in his insights and preparedness to be available to the person. Most counsellees I have known, who have deep problems with self-acceptance, will assume that they are being a nuisance, that they are wasting the counsellor's time and the counsellor would prefer to be doing something else or involved in "more important things". The sense of worthlessness is very pervasive and the counsellee will have great difficulty in accepting that the counsellor is even concerned. When that penny drops, he has other things to face, which are a good deal more painful.

He will have to face himself and he will have to learn what it means to deny himself. We will spend the next chapter looking at penitence and its place in counselling (it is very central), but let us simply note here that recognition of sin, while it may be a terrible thing to face, is the only way to self-denial and therefore salvation. Nobody likes seeing himself in terms of his own sin – he prefers to look at more beautiful, if artificial, sights. But, unless he is prepared to see himself as he is, which is the only way that God sees him, he cannot accept himself. It is in the denying of the things which really seem important to him that the Cross becomes effective and the Resurrection a reality in his life.

I have had so many people who have come to the point of facing themselves, or some aspect of themselves of which they are guilty, repulsed or afraid, or all three. The good news is that, with the loving support of the counsellor and in prayer and the presence of the Spirit of God, they have broken the fear barrier and looked and seen the true person, and known in the moment of pure fear, the incredible realisation that they are still loved. That is denial of self, that is what Paul means about crucifying the old man, that is what it means to start loving oneself.

I must end this chapter by saying something about *community and self-acceptance*. I have a deep worry about the counsellor who works outside the Christian community. If he does, he is caught in a terrible trap, unless he is superhuman. He will have to "succeed" – in other words, more or less guarantee results – for he will be dependent upon his own reputation for further clients. He will also be dependent on his own resources and be he never so skilled, competent and holy, he will not have them all. But, worst of all, unless he is very careful, he will believe that he can "go it alone", and that will soon mean without the Holy Spirit to guide and direct him. No counsellor has all the skills and abilities needed. If he is part of a community, he will be able to draw on others' skills for the benefit of the counsellee. He will know where he is not strong or where his gifts do not stretch. He will not try to "hog people to himself" in order to justify himself. He will gladly help the person to one better able to help.

I have a beloved colleague at St Paul's, with whom over the years I have been able to build an incredibly effective ministry of counselling and healing. Many is the time when I have sent someone, with whom I have been very involved, to him, knowing that, at that point, and for that area of concern, he is the person whose gifts and insights in the Lord are most likely to help. Increasingly on the staff, we pray and discuss who is the best person to help Student X, or if he is going to another member of staff, does that member feel that God is calling him to continue with Student X. That way, Student X gets the best possible care and is helped to grow to a self-acceptance very much more effectively. Trust of each other in that way allows the gifts in the body to be used to God's glory, without pride or jealousy. There is no place for pride or selfishness or jealousy in the counselling ministry, for the person who suffers most is the counsellee.

The other side of community is also critical. It may be that the counsellee comes to a measure of self-acceptance, but if he is not linked to an accepting community, all the counselling in the world will be to no avail. I was very moved, many years ago, when a visitor to the college told a story of a young, unmarried, pregnant girl, crippled with guilt and thrown out of her own home, who found her way to this person's home. There she stayed until her confinement, which was very difficult, and was followed by major complications, resulting in her being in hospital for several weeks. During her stay at the speaker's home, John, the speaker, had not been able to help her past her guilt to any degree of self-acceptance. After she had been taken to hospital, John phoned two young girls in his parish, both of whom worked as secretaries in the city. All he said was, "Jane is in hospital and there are complications." For all the time that "Jane" was in hospital, those two visited her every day, including Sunday. That meant catching two buses each way after work, giving up most of their social life for that time and putting themselves to considerable inconvenience over an extended period. It was those two girls who, by their loving, self-denying acceptance, helped "Jane" to a new awareness of herself as an object of love – worth something in their eyes and therefore acceptable in her own eyes. Of course, John went to see her, but the involvement of these two girls as part of the accepting community was at the heart of any real ongoing self-acceptance for "Jane".

Enough said? Possibly. But the opposite is also true. As a parish priest, I went to see a man who was a well-known, wild member of the community, and got him to the point of recognising his sin and wanting to change. The parish was a small and very loving one and I knew that he would be accepted if he started to come and worship, which was his great desire. He was afraid, however, for he felt that he would be laughed at. I reassured him that that would not happen. So, the next Sunday, he duly arrived. I made sure I was there when he did so. One of the sidesmen on duty looked up, saw him and, quite involuntarily, said, "Good gracious, what are *you* doing here?" The man turned, looked at me and left the church, never to return. I nearly cried and today, twenty years later, I can still see the look in his eyes, as they said, "I told you so – I *am* unworthy and unaccepted." The Church, the body of Christ, exists to express the love of Christ, to help people to a self-acceptance in him, which makes it possible to be whole in God and in relation to others.

In my own deeply divided land, the same need is true within

society. As whites and blacks learn to look at each other and neither fear, nor hate, but see and love, they will help each other to new degrees of self-acceptance and of the love of Christ, which knows no such division. I know, because I have experienced that type of love in this sad land of ours, and it has helped me to become a more whole and self-accepting person. The Church as a community can do the same.

Chapter
7

Repentance and Forgiveness

Perhaps the hardest things that we have to do in our lives are summed up in the two words which are in the title of this chapter, "Repent" and "Forgive". Repentance implies a number of things. For a start, it means the sort of dependence which most of us reject, for reasons we will look at in a while. It also means that we accept the responsibility implicit in admitting that we are sinners who have made a mess of our own lives and a considerable mess of other people's as well. To accept that sort of responsibility implies the need to turn and focus our lives in a new direction. Unfortunately, if you are anything like me, it is not possible to do that on one's own, for I have neither the will power, nor the strength, even when I have the desire to do it. I need a saviour, one on whose strength I can rely, so that in turning to him, I am turning to God. I also need a saviour who continues to sustain me when things are rough. So I need the Holy Spirit, the sustaining power of God unfettered to time and space, who keeps me focused on Jesus – or attempts to.

If we want to think of it in terms of a biblical picture we have already seen, we are like the blind beggar, Bartimaeus,[1] standing naked and helpless but expectant before Jesus. Repentance requires recognising our own helpless dependence and accepting that we are blind, naked beggars in need of sight. Then it is possible for us after receiving our sight, to follow him on the Way. Repentance is a painful experience, for it feels humiliating, but it is the first step towards the wholeness which Jesus promises us.

Repentance is only part of the problem. Forgiveness is the

other part. Repentance is the process or attitude of being brought to the mercy of God and, in dependence on him, accepting his forgiveness. So having repented and received forgiveness, we are also to exercise forgiveness in our relationship with others. As we shall see, a significant section of Jesus's teaching, including a section of the prayer Our Lord taught us, sees *our* forgiveness as critical in our relationships with God and our fellow man.

All of this presupposes the reality of sin. Sin is the active putting of ourselves at the centre of life and, as a result, putting God anywhere other than at the centre. It is a state, like poison in the system; it is only when sores start to appear that we are aware that the system has been poisoned. If we become obsessed by the sores, we are not actually facing the real problem. If we only treat the sores, the poison remains in the system. It may be that one of the sores becomes so big and inflamed that we can only see and feel that one. If that is the case, of course we have to treat it and hopefully eradicate it. But that, while it may feel wonderful, does not solve the problem, for it is not the problem. The poison still flows actively through the system. Obviously what is needed is to treat the condition, not the symptoms, and to affect a wholeness to the complete body, not just part of it.

Many is the time that the counsellor will see the signs of sin and disease in a person's life but, while he will have to take these seriously, he will be foolish if he thinks that they are the real problems. He needs to help the person to bring his whole condition under the healing light of Christ. So, sin affects every aspect of life and, from the counselling point of view, it is as well to remind ourselves what sin does.

Covering up

It is *very* difficult to accept sin in ourselves, so either we try to cover it, in the hope that others will not see it, or we attempt to shift the blame. The process of lying, or exaggerating, is part of the cover up, and worse still, is a deliberate attempt to lay the blame on someone wholly innocent. Often it is not as crass as that. It is where we put the emphasis or *how* we tell the story. Anyone having had to do with marriage counselling will know that there is virtually no such thing as an "innocent party". (In twenty-five years, I have only come across one divorce where I believe the one party was genuinely without blame.) Yet if one listens to each of the partners talking, one would imagine that, while it is conceded that there might be minor faults here and there, each of the partners sees herself or himself as innocent – and injured. If one unpacks the "minor faults", one usually discovers a can of worms!

So sin covers up and as long as it does so, there can be no repentance; in fact, many people seem to believe that no sin exists if it is undetected. In which case, the sin is that of being discovered! As with Bartimaeus, it is only when we throw off the mean rags which we clutch so tightly to us and are prepared to be seen for what we are, that repentance and forgiveness can become a reality.

Ignorance

One of the great cries of people who have made a mess of things is "I didn't know", "I didn't realise", "I didn't understand". That may be so, but it does not mean that it is any less sinful. Ignorance is one of the major spreaders of sin. Sin does not have to be deliberate in order to be sinful. It may be that there is less blame if a person does not know what he has done, or been, but that does not make the consequences easier or less sinful. I umpire hockey and one of the things that players have to learn and accept is that a foul is a foul, whether it was intentional or not. If it is intentional, the penalties are much more severe – that is the only difference. In practice, most of the fouls *are* unintentional, but that does not mean they are less of a problem to the opposition.

So ignorance has widespread problems. I came across a girl who was pregnant and who had honestly believed that she could not become pregnant if she did not have a climax. She was happily sleeping with her boyfriends and studiously avoiding climaxes so as to avoid pregnancy. The fact of her pregnancy was a terrible shock to her! That is sinful, naive and ignorant – but she acted on it.

Doctors who have worked in rural and underdeveloped parts of the world say that the worst problems relating to health are caused by ignorance. People who drink polluted water because it tastes better, people who feed their children the wrong foods because they think they are good for them, the list is endless, the ignorance invincible. The same is true in agriculture and other basic areas of human existence. But disease, malnutrition and consequent debilitation of life is an expression of sin, even when ignorance is the cause.

Other people's sin

There are areas where people are the innocent victims of other people's sin. One of the things which I have come to be aware of in counselling is how vulnerable children are. The frustrated mother who batters her child in a fit of frenzy; the children begotten in selfish sinfulness and left to fend for themselves; the children who are the victims of jealousy, anger, fear and the whole range of destructive human emotions. I had a person come to see me once, who was very insecure. It became clear that at a stage in his life the family was moving and he had an old toy which was a symbol of security in a situation where he loved his grandfather, but was frightened of the sharp and sarcastic tongue of his father. When the move came, he asked his grandfather if he could keep his toy and he had been told he could. But his father had taken the toy away from the screaming child and said, "We don't want to take any junk like that." Nearly forty years later, that terrible experience, covered over the years, was still pouring poison into the system and he was still not getting on well with his father. So often we are victims of the sin of others, no matter how it comes at us. The wounds of those experiences last a lifetime, unless they are exposed to the healing presence of our Lord Jesus.

Deliberate sin

We must be careful, as counsellors, not to avoid the deliberateness of sin – that would be stupid. There is a tendency in some circles to play down sin in any form or, worse still, explain it away. It seems to me that the value of Jay Adams[2] is that he insists on the reality of sin. My problem with him is that he seems to want to see sin in a rather restricted way and I am sure that is not the whole biblical picture.

Sin is nevertheless *the* potent force in the human condition and we would be silly if we did not believe that an awful lot of the human situation was brought about by deliberate wilful sin, whether it is cold-blooded or of the more steamy variety. I am not thinking of the obvious criminal sins such as murder, rather of the deliberate extortion of others, the way in which the life is squeezed out of others through exploitation, the way people are victimised through jealousy or fear. In all of this, the counsellor, as we shall see, has to discern what is sin, and help him to repentance and the acceptance of forgiveness.

Jesus's teaching on repentance and forgiveness

Repentance
If we take the pattern of the Gospels seriously, then Jesus's teaching starts as a follow up to John the Baptist's. Thus, John is reported by Mark and Luke as "preaching a baptism of repentance for the forgiveness of sins".[3] So, it is not surprising that, after John's imprisonment, Jesus appears to carry on John's work, though with a new dimension. He comes preaching "the Kingdom of God is at hand; repent and believe in the Gospel".[4] Thus, at the heart of the Gospel which Jesus proclaims is the need for repentance, a change of heart, a new direction. It is the recognition of a new set of

values and the desire and preparedness to live by them. So, the Kingdom of God cannot be entered until there is a changed attitude on the part of the one who desires to enter it. That, incidentally, gives the lie to the sort of attitude which somehow believes that entry into the Kingdom of God is a right automatically bestowed on anyone with the right nationality, denominational membership or even a member of the Church itself or Church affiliation.

Certainly repentance is necessary for any real relationship with God and one's fellows. In the Old Testament, the archetype would be Job, who, while righteous by every tenet of his religion, is only able to come to a proper relationship with God when he gets beyond religion to a face to face confrontation with him. At that point, he repents and all else falls into place. So, too, the Gospels make it clear that it is only when we see Jesus for who he is and respond to him as Lord, that we are in a position to repent and then follow him.

So the sinner who repents is the one who causes the most joy in Heaven,[5] more we are told than the ninety-nine who need no repentance. Given the context of that saying, Jesus appears to be saying, as he says so often, that the righteous are in fact the self-righteous, who actually need to repent, but cannot see the necessity to do so.

The parables of Jesus are full of the need for repentance and the consequences of it. The obvious example is the Prodigal Son.[6] The son has to "come to himself"[7] and when he does, he gets up and deliberately does two things. First he returns home, and second, he acknowledges his sinfulness. Both of these constitute repentance; together they affirm his need for new life, which is the end product of repentance. Zacchaeus repents[8] and, as a result, "Salvation has come to this house."

In so many cases the parables point to a turning to a new life and a new-found joy which is certainly reflected in Heaven. The Sermon on the Mount is full of many instances of turning and a new beginning. The point of "the hypocrites",[9] or "the Gentiles"[10] who, while being terribly religious, are in fact very worldly – and whose piety is paraded for the world to see and admire.

The life of repentance by contrast is that in which the piety is not shown, but the new behaviour is, and it is that which makes the difference. Jeremias[11] makes a persuasive point that the saying of Jesus concerning "becoming like children",[12] which is rendered by the RSV as "unless you turn and become like children, you will never enter the Kingdom of Heaven", should be translated: "unless you become like children again, you will not reach the basileia (kingdom) of God." He would interpret this saying as "learning to say 'Abba' again"[13] – in other words, when we have once more achieved the dependence on God which a child has on a reliable and loving father. So the prodigal son returns home and in the returning trusts his father to accept him, even when he acknowledges his own sinful rejection of his father.

So we could go on. Perhaps the saddest event in the Gospels is that of the rich man who wanted to follow, who wanted to "inherit eternal life", but for whom the price was too high.[14] The sadness with which he turned away is at least an honest reaction, but his riches made it impossible for him to repent. They were a stumbling block to the new life of repentance and faith. Those of us who are wealthy may well have to wrestle with Jesus's injunction to that rich man, for I suspect that most of us want to follow Jesus, provided we are allowed to travel heavy. We follow with a removal van, carrying all we dare not let go, behind us as security. Jesus points out that repentance is the process of getting rid of the false securities and following him, even when it looks like a very fearful possibility. So, the good news of Jesus, for which Jesus calls us to repent and believe, may feel to many like very bad news, and if we look at it hard, makes for great insecurity by the world's standards. Trust in God is fine in theory – the practice is rather different!

Forgiveness
In the teaching in the Sermon on the Mount on repentance

and doing things differently, there comes the Lord's Prayer with its injunctions to forgive as the Father forgives. It is clear from the verses following[15] that forgiveness is understood as being conditional. The repentance of which we have spoken and which is summed up in the petition for forgiveness in the Lord's Prayer is of no avail if it is not balanced by a real desire and preparedness to forgive others. The turning to God must accompany an overflowing awareness of the other person and an equal desire to forgive him the sins, debts, trespasses (you can take your pick according to your favourite translation) which he has inflicted upon you. In any case, the sort of debt he is likely to owe you is of no value at all compared to the debt which you owe to God. So in the Lord's Prayer the intention, at least as Matthew gives it to us (Luke gives us a much shorter version in a very different context), is conditional. The implication seems to be something like this: "Forgive us our debts in the same measure as we are prepared to forgive those who owe us anything." This attitude seems to be borne out in another part of Matthew's Gospel, when Peter, in a fit of overwhelming piety, suggests that seven times is a more than generous number of times to forgive anyone who has sinned against him.[16] Peter, it seems, was stretching forgiveness to the limit, but Jesus will have no limit, that surely is the significance of "seventy times seven". That is for one person, not all together! In other words, forgiveness is at the heart of our relationship with God; to know that we are forgiven means that we in turn are able to forgive others with a similar generosity. The point is simple. It is relatively easy to forgive once, seven times is almost impossible; seventy times seven requires a different attitude to life; an attitude of humility and a dependence upon God who has already forgiven you a debt so huge that it is beyond computing.

In Luke[17] the equivalent of the saying in Matthew comes with a group of teachings on "temptation", or more probably, persecution. This puts forgiveness in an even more dramatic setting. Sin is to be rebuked and repentance accepted as many times as sin and repentance happen. And the sinner is the persecutor! No wonder the disciples asked for an increase of faith – how else could they cope with that expectation of forgiveness?[18]

Obviously the most significant teaching on forgiveness is that of the unforgiving servant.[19] Following as it does on Peter's suggestion of seven times as being adequate forgiveness, Jesus puts it in proportion: approximately a million to one; in other words beyond reckoning. The one who so effectively pleaded his cause for the huge amount, seemed still to need to retain his authority and power over his brother servant in a very tiny area and for a very small amount. At issue is not so much the amounts, as the attitudes. The generous and forgiving king can at least expect a similar response from the one who owed so much. So it is with God. The nature of sin is such that when he forgives us our sin, an overwhelming and unpayable debt is released; but that debt can only be effectively released as the freed debtor treats his fellow man in a similar way with regard to the minuscule debts which accrue from that direction.

Notice, too, that this parable is one which shows us the nature of the Kingdom. The Kingdom requires the attitude of forgiveness indicated in the parable. The forgiving heart is counterbalanced by the penitent one; both are necessary for wholeness and salvation.

Jesus's forgiveness

The Gospels make it quite clear that only the Son of Man can forgive sins[20] and in Jesus's ministry the forgiveness of sins is the first step in ushering in the Kingdom of God, thereby freeing men from the bondage of Satan. Sickness, demon possession, disease, hardness of heart – these are the areas where Satan rules supreme. By breaking the power of sin, the kingdom of Satan is put to flight. Forgiveness of sin is therefore much more than simply saying sorry. It is release from bondage; the first step in the new life.

So the paralytic who is able to walk, the leper who is

cleansed, the demoniac who is exorcised, the sick person who
is healed, all are beneficiaries of Jesus's forgiving presence,
breaking the power of sin. In each case, the person is penitent, in that he recognises the authority of God and is
dependent upon Jesus to exercise that authority. The fascinating counterpoint to the parable of the unjust servant is the
parable which Jesus told to Simon the Pharisee.[21] The incident which gave rise to the parable is one which we shall look
at in more detail in a later chapter, but here we need only note
that a woman who was presumably a rehabilitated (or not?)
prostitute, had wet his feet with her tears and anointed them
with ointment. Simon's complaint was that by inference Jesus
was being defiled by the woman. The whole incident would
have been utterly repugnant to the Pharisee. Jesus's response
is to tell a story – very simply – of two people who are
released from their debts. Who is the more grateful? *Answer*:
he who owed more. *Inference*: this woman has more to be
grateful for than you, for she is a more obvious sinner. In
forgiving her sins, Jesus gives her new life – but that does not
mean that she can go on sinning. What it does mean is that
forgiveness is something which is Jesus's main function – to
help people to a new relationship with God. Jesus makes that
clear when he points out that he has come quite specifically to
"call . . . the sinners". There is no need for those who have no
awareness of the need for forgiveness to ask for it, but the
implicit judgment in that remark stands as an anvil on which
even the hardest of hearts will hopefully become pliant.

So the forgiving love of Jesus is always available for those
who need to be forgiven. Even in the worst circumstances, he
is able to forgive. As he is nailed to the Cross, he lives out the
reality of "until seventy times seven". As he utters the words
"Father forgive them", he is showing the way to new life, in
the face of persecution and blinding pain. That is the attitude
which he expects of us, and it is not surprising that Stephen
the first martyr already reflected precisely the same loving
forgiving concern which is the mark of the follower of Jesus.[22]

Even then we are not finished. The Cross itself, the whole

ghastly process of the Passion is such that, as Jesus absorbs the sin of man, he lives out the saving forgiveness of God. So in Ephesians, Paul tells us: "In him we have redemption through his blood, the forgiveness of our trespasses, according to the riches of his grace, which he lavished upon us."[23] In Colossians he writes: "he has delivered us from the dominion of darkness and transferred us to the kingdom of his beloved Son, in whom we have redemption, the forgiveness of sins."[24] Forgiveness of sins is at least one of the purposes of the Cross – and it is in the Cross that we glory.

Repentance and forgiveness in counselling

It may seem that I have somewhat laboured the obvious in this chapter. I make no apology if I have. It is critical in counselling that we take this very seriously. Where there is no penitence and forgiveness there is no salvation. And if there is no salvation, then is our counselling to no advantage. So let us look at repentance and forgiveness in the counselling process.

The Cross is the focal point of repentance

If we take the Cross seriously, we will soon become aware that it is a terrible stumbling block to many who seek counselling. The very fact that we have a Saviour who dies for us and calls us to turn and follow him is not what many want. The Cross implies the pain of sin and with it comes the fear of seeing sin for what it really is – the rejection of God and our fellow man, as well as the more profound rejection of ourselves. So, as we saw in the earlier part of this chapter, we would prefer to pass the buck, or cover up, or focus the sin on someone else.

Essentially, much counselling begins at least with the client not wanting the Cross, preferring a man-made answer or something akin to a baby's dummy to keep him happy. The Cross stands, however, as the measure of our sin, be it deliberate, ignorant or the innocent victim type. The Cross is man's response to God's love and God's answer – Father, forgive. But it is more; it is also the means whereby we can face sin and in the resultant penitence receive forgiveness. Even that does not say it fully. Penitence has an element of risk. If we want to go back to Genesis, it is the risk of being, as it were, naked and unashamed, which is presented to us. When we repent we are most vulnerable – and most open to the possibility of being pulled either back into the kingdom of evil, or into the kingdom of God. That is where the Cross gives hope. For naked and faithful, Jesus gives us the key to new life, as he lives out the forgiveness of God. Penitence has the risk of acceptance or rejection; the Cross assures us of acceptance, which is, after all, what forgiveness is.

Jesus shows us the need for repentance

Most of the people I have counselled know that they are sinners. In fact, most of them have such a poor self-image that they have a terrible fear of anyone seeing them as they really are. But they also have built-in mechanisms which seek to avoid the need for repentance. We have seen these in the earlier part of the chapter. So it is a sort of yes–no situation. They want to repent, but they fear it terribly.

If we look at Jesus – in his teaching and his relationships – we see that there is a strong reassurance that, while repentance may be painful, it is always necessary and, where it is affected, it is always joyful. So it is with the prodigal son, and the sinner who prays for forgiveness in the temple and goes away justified. The finding of the sheep and the coin give rise to joy – a similar joy is expressed in Heaven for one penitent sinner.

More important, however, Jesus shows us that life without penitence is a deformed and inadequate expression of the loving fulness of life, which he offers to people as they come under the sovereignty of God or, if you like, enter the Kingdom of Heaven. The wonder of the Kingdom is that it gives us the unity with God, the unity within ourselves, with others and in creation which is depicted in Genesis. Repentance makes it possible to turn to God again and live within the richness of that unifying relationship. So repentance is the first step in the restoration of man into the full image and likeness of God. And forgiveness is God's loving acceptance of the sinner.

If all this sounds like a lecture on evangelism, then that is fine, for it must be. Counselling always has that element of evangelism. The Christian counsellor is concerned to mirror the loving presence of God into people's lives in such a way that they are prepared to take the risk and turn to him, which is, after all, repentance. So when Peter had delivered his famous sermon in Jerusalem,[25] the people having been "cut to the heart" ask what the next step was. Peter's reply was direct and uncompromising. "Repent and be baptised everyone in the name of Jesus Christ for the forgiveness of your sins."[26] That, of course, is the heart of evangelism – as it is the heart of counselling. It is learning to say "Abba", and learning that God is the healer if we want to be made whole; but that he heals on his condition, not ours.

At the beginning of the chapter, I mentioned that sin is like poison in the body, causing sores, which may or may not have to be treated separately. Repentance is first of all seeing past the symptoms to the true condition and then desiring to be cured. I had a person come to me who could not sleep well. I have no real experience with dreams or their interpretation, but it did seem that the recurrence of a particular theme in the dreams was indicative of a state well beyond insomnia. It took a while, but we were able to get to the heart of the problem: a deep rooted feeling of inadequacy which, strangely, he thought he had dealt with. It was still there, however, manifesting itself in what, for him, was a rather unlikely way. Repentance in that context meant learning to trust God's love, so that the feelings of anger and pain engendered by one of his parents would be overcome by God's forgiveness of him and them, and likewise his forgiveness of his parents. It was like a bursting bubble – much came out, but with it came an awareness of the forgiving presence of God, which has seldom left him.

Revenge and grudges and spiritism

The most obvious area of counselling in which repentance is overtly called for is in the desire for revenge, the harbouring of grudges and involvement in the occult.

Revenge is the desire to get one's own back. The Old Testament rule of "an eye for an eye" is an attempt to stop people exacting greater punishment than the crime calls for. It is in fact a very human rule, caring for the injured as well as the guilty. Jesus forces us to look further, to attitudes of revenge, to unspoken hostilities, which desire a crushing of the other person. At that stage, the one who feels injured is himself deformed, for the desire for revenge, however it is felt or expressed, crushes him and turns him into a person obsessed. Everything is seen through that filter and everything the object of revenge does will be interpreted as further evidence of his malevolence.

A person came to me on one occasion with just such a problem: it was quite literally eating him away. He was morose, angry, unable to relate to anyone, for they were somehow pulled into his web of suspicion and desire for revenge. The only acceptable people were those who also disliked the person he disliked. He had an ulcer and hypertension – a real mess. His doctor had given him tranquillisers and those had probably saved him from a heart attack.

He went back in his memory to the incidents which had given rise to the feelings with which he now lived. It was very dramatic and, in some ways, quite amusing. He saw the scene again and then he saw Jesus quite clearly walk up to the person whom he disliked so much and put his arm around him. The client was so astonished and humbled that he started to cry very quietly. He saw for the first time what he could not see before – that Jesus loved the other too. Strangely, he learned from that situation that he also was beloved of God.

Of course, it was not as easy as that. It took time, but that first vision was enough of the antidote of love for him to face the love of the Cross, come to a real repentance and even in time to make contact with the other person and forgive and be forgiven.

In a way, I hate giving these examples, for they sound simple and so easy. They are not; behind that story was much trauma and a lot of time and a great deal of emotional agonising – to say nothing of some dead ends. But God is a loving god and he wanted that person's healing as much as the person who had come to the end of his tether wanted it. Revenge and the desire for it may have its origin in justifiable reactions to feelings of rejection, but it still requires repentance and forgiveness.

Grudges. This is very similar to revenge in many ways. It is perhaps not quite as aggressive or emotion-consuming. While revenge may be like a raging abscess, the harbouring of a grudge is like a quietly growing cancer – just as deadly. I lived with just such a condition for many years, vaguely aware of the disease, but not really prepared to look too closely, not in fact wanting to. The point was that the grudge was as a result of an exchange, during a conversation with a friend. He was certainly unaware of what he had said or done. The grudge grew quietly, occasionally showing me that it was there. Each time it manifested itself, I simply tried to push it further under the surface, where the rot continued.

It was only when, years later, I hit a crisis and could no longer avoid it that I realised that it had corroded almost all my relationships. My personality had changed, I tried to hide the feelings of rejection behind a brash and conceited manner, which was as false as anything I have ever come up with. To this day, the results of that are a deep sense of inadequacy in one or two specific areas. The grudge could have been dealt with in five minutes at the time, if I had simply tried to express my feelings within a day or two of the event. But no, pride guaranteed that that did not happen and, many years later, I turned to a friend and colleague for help. He, wise and loving man, helped me to see the root and, in a horror of what a monster I had unwittingly and sinfully created, I turned to our Lord in penitence, finding the forgiveness which only he can give. The fact that it was a formal confession in front of this friend, who, in his capacity as priest, pronounced absolution and forgiveness, in no way made it less the forgiveness of God. In fact the formality was crucial. There is great assurance as God works through the offices of his Church.

The point is simple. The initial pain was certainly genuine; the grudge was sinful. For there to be healing, there had to be penitence and reconciliation in so far as that was possible. Sometimes the object of the grudge is long since dead, but the person harbouring the grudge has still to forgive – and forget. Forgetting too is essential. No forgetting – no forgiveness. Continuing to remember and dwell on the grudge, even if it is unconscious at times, causes the cancer. The counsellor's task is to help find where the cancer is and help the person to penitence and forgiveness.

The occult. I have no great experience in this area. What I have confirms what I have learnt from others, namely that indulging in even apparently innocent activities such as ouija boards, glassy-glassy and tarot cards can open one to the demonic forces. It is only a very short step from this to a very specific pattern of sexual indulgence and aberrations and then deeper into the occult itself. It seems that if one deliberately puts oneself in the area of Satan's power, he will be quick to grab one and pull one further in. As with all sin and evil, it starts with apparently innocent activities, but with it come demonic possession of which the person may not be aware.

In other cases, demonic possession can come through deliberate and perverse sinfulness, often with attitudes which mock and scorn those who are in authority over them. In these cases, the first step to a restored life involves a specific confession of sins and a formal renunciation of the satanic forces with which the person has become involved. Only then can exorcism take place and it must be done under the authority of one licensed to perform that ministry and no other, unless there is an emergency. If the latter happens, the matter must be reported to a Church authority. There is no place in the Christian ministry for people simply doing their own thing – worse still, seeing demonic possession in every situation.

One of the incidents which made me more angry in my ministry than almost any other has ever done, was when I had been working with a person who had been, rightly in my view, diagnosed as schizophrenic. He was an outpatient of a mental institution and, after many months of regular treatment, visiting, prayer and much loving help, he was starting to make real progress. At that point, he went and consulted a new minister in town. This man listened to the patient for perhaps fifteen minutes, declared him to be possessed and proceeded to "exorcise" him, putting the patient back to a worse condition than he had been before. I still find myself almost unbelievably angry when I think of it. Apart from being entirely unauthorised, he blundered into a situation on the basis of a number of presuppositions, did not bother to check them out, and with incredible irresponsibility, could have done even more harm than he did. Fortunately, there were people to pick up the wreck which he had left behind.

There was a horrifying incident a few years ago when shortly after a person who was clearly psychotic had been "exorcised", he went home and brutally murdered his wife. When dealing with people we can never take chances in this way. If we are not skilled, or do not have the knowledge, we have no right to make assumptions without specialist insights. The medical profession is an incredible gift from God. There is no greater arrogance on the part of the counsellor than when, for whatever reason, he chooses to disregard it to make his own assumptions. My experience is that the medical profession is only too prepared to listen to suggestions and insights; it does not take kindly to people who, with no training, act as though they know everything. When exorcism is necessary there are certain things which we must bear in mind.

(*a*) Look for demon possession last, even if there are signs which indicate that it is present.

(*b*) Insist on a formal confession as part of the process. Without it the patient may somehow go through the motions of penitence without actually being penitent.

(*c*) After the demon has come out – and it must be ordered out in the name of Jesus – insist on praying for the infilling of the Spirit of God. *In that context* wait for "tongues" to manifest itself as a sure sign of the presence of the Spirit.[27] Take seriously what our Lord said about "the last state being worse than the first". If the Holy Spirit does not fill the void then be assured that the demonic powers will.

(*d*) The exorcised person needs a great deal of support and protection afterwards; he needs to be placed in a family or community where he can be sustained during the next few weeks. Temptations will be very powerful as Satan attempts to re-win him.

(*e*) Pray for protection and discernment for yourself. You will need it.

The Prodigal Son Syndrome. That is my name for it, but it is very important in counselling. The counsellor is frequently faced with people who have been pushed into an interview, or may even have come of their own will, but who are not penitent, have no desire to come to terms with anything and who are at the best uninterested and, at the worst, rebellious and unco-operative. They may be people whose families have exerted pressure on them, or, more likely, they are people known in a pastoral situation who want nothing to do with the Church and "all those hypocrites". Whatever may be the case, the person is set on going his own way and doing what he wants.

If that is the case, let him go. Your responsibility will be to minister to the family that they may lovingly let him go and not say "I told you so" when he falls – which he will do. If pressure is put on him to conform, he may do so for a while, but eventually he will rebel so violently that when the break comes, he will go for good and the pain of that break will be more terrible than we can imagine.

Many is the time that a couple have married because one or other set of parents has disapproved and exerted such pressure on them not to, that in reality that has pushed the couple closer together. In that situation, the couple cannot see each other clearly. They are only aware of the need to protect their own identity and their pride will not allow them to be pushed around. The result is that after the marriage, the faults and incompatibility which they ought to and would have seen, had they been unpressured during the time of courtship, come to the fore. Then, so often, they either live in a hell relationship, or they divorce, which is even more traumatic than they thought possible.

The point about the prodigal son is that the father allowed him the freedom to do what he thought right and loved him, even when he was at his most unlovable. The living death gave way to a new life of repentance, forgiveness, acceptance and security. The Alcoholics Anonymous movement have an awareness that, unless a person comes to the point of knowing that he is a slave to alcohol, there is no point in trying to help him, for his pride keeps telling him that he can still control it. So they let him hit the bottom, when he has lost everything, then it may be that he will realise that he needs "a power greater than himself" and repent – turn, seek help and be saved. The same is true of sin. It is only when the person realises that he cannot cope, when his pride is in shreds and his relationships in tatters, that he will repent and be saved. And the attitude of the Church? That must always be the same: it must be forgiveness "until seventy times seven", never ending.

Chapter
8

Giving and Receiving

This chapter is concerned with dependencies. It is inevitable and right that we should have dependencies in our lives. The baby is dependent on its mother in the womb and develops the type of dependency which will make or break it as a person during the first months of its life. The child becomes dependent physically for food and drink, as well as for love and acceptance. Where these are not present, the child will wither in some form and have to rely on others. There is nothing wrong with that; without other people we would not be able to survive. The Genesis account of creation is quite clear that "it is not good that man should be alone"[1] and man is at his best generally, not as a hermit but within the ever widening circles of the family and society. I come from a very loving family with five children. My parents managed to show us such love that a friend of my sisters once complained that "the Buchanans are the only family of five children where each one behaves like a spoilt only child"! On reflection, that is something of a compliment to my parents, though I doubt whether they took it as such; I certainly never asked!

Guy Butler, a man of considerable reputation as a poet, teacher and scholar, has recently published two fascinating volumes of autobiography.[2] The first, *Karoo Morning*, deals with the years prior to his going to university. In this delightful piece of writing, he manages to show that his own family was surrounded by a large number of relatives who formed a fabric of considerable strength. His sense of identity and the strength of his own personality was shaped on the one hand by the interaction of parents and brothers and sisters, and on the other by the more varied relationships with grandparents, aunts, uncles and a large number of cousins, whom he seemed to keep discovering. Without them all, it is clear that his personality would have been considerably impoverished. As it is, he is a person of great character, who has enriched the lives of many by his scholarship and faith.

Dependencies are good; they are part of the fabric of life and much joy of life is gained from relationships which have been savoured over many years. Marriages are made of the same stuff. An interdependency can be created so that when things go well, the couple is somehow bigger than the two individuals concerned. The giving and receiving in such a relationship is essential to each other – the couple complement each other and if the relationship can be achieved without threat, one-sidedness or jealousy, then the two people not only grow as a couple, but are wonderfully able to express their individuality as well. That is the Christian ideal expressed by Paul when he instructs husbands and wives to "be subject to one another out of reverence for Christ".[3] We do not need relationships where one dominates the other, nor do we need what Hurding describes (with delightful diagrams to go with it) as "lean-to marriages".[4] The essential and joyful expression of life is one of giving and receiving. And that is where the difficulties lie. Many people are so insecure that they dare not give, some so insecure that they cannot receive. Clergy are very frequently in the latter category – we are so used to giving that we are afraid that receiving will somehow expose us as being weak. Worse still, receiving implies dependence, which is also not acceptable. We too have our pride! There are many people in my country who have been beggarised: they assume that whatever they need will be given and they are prepared to give nothing of what little they have, of time or anything else. Perhaps "prepared" is too strong a word. It is more likely that over the generations they have been put in a position where they have not been allowed to give and now do not believe it is necessary.

Whatever the situation, giving and receiving are the two

most difficult things in life. What if we are asked to give when we believe we have nothing to give? Or to give in areas where we know or feel impoverished? (Poverty is not only economic, it is just as virulent spiritually, emotionally and socially.) What if we are always on the receiving end – be it of anger, handouts, or even decisions made for us (decisions which can be political or made by dominant parents or spouse or even well-meaning friends)? Giving and receiving are essential for good relationships.

In counselling there are two different giving and receiving dynamics at work:

1. Helping the counsellee to give and receive after the manner and in the strength of Jesus.
2. The counsellor's acceptance that in the counselling relationship there must also be a giving and receiving.

Many counsellors believe that their task is to give; they do not expect to receive anything in the process. I can only say that, apart from many startling insights I have gained, I have also received the most undeserved love from counsellees, who in areas where I am weak, have been strong. I have learned to accept that gratefully, to say nothing of the joy of receiving and being the object of pure affection and love, which can last many years. This is not infatuation or a one-sided dependency. It derives from two people interacting and seeking the way of Christ who is the ultimate giver of all good things. The result is a life greatly enriched from having learned to receive as well as give.

There is an interesting little saying of Jesus which does not come in the Gospels. Paul, on his way to Jerusalem, meets the elders of Ephesus and bids them farewell in a most moving speech. He ends by saying: "In all things I have shown you that by so toiling one must help the weak, remembering the words of our Lord Jesus 'It is more blessed to give than to receive'."[5] Strangely, this saying is not reflected in the Gospels, but it does sum up at least one aspect of ministry and counselling. I have always felt, however, that our Lord would have wanted also to balance that by suggesting perhaps that "It is as blessed to receive as to give". We need them both and we only have to look at Jesus's teaching and his life to realise that both play an enormous part in his ministry. He taught people to give and receive, and was prepared to do the same in his relationships with others – he allowed others the joy of giving to him as well as receiving from him.

Giving and receiving in Jesus's teaching

Giving

At the centre of Jesus's teaching is a "giving God" – a God who expresses his love by giving. That is not distractive to Jesus: in the Old Testament, God takes his initiative to give – a partner for Adam, authority over creation, clothes of skin after the Fall; he gives Abraham a son and a heritage, a wife for Isaac, a covenant for Israel, a land for his people. Leaders, judges, kings and prophets – all are given. Nothing that Israel does deserves his love and goodness. He has chosen Israel because he desires to equip them to be his people – to be the agent whereby the other nations are brought into that relationship which he desires for all. He is a God who gives, because that is the nature of his love. As a result, his people are to be givers too. That emerges in Jesus's teaching. He comes "preaching", which is itself a form of giving. What he preached was: "repent and believe", which are giving responses, for they require a turning away from self and giving of one's whole being to God. Jesus makes it clear that he came to "give his life as a ransom for many".[6] That is very explicit; the nature of God's giving is total and all-embracing. There is no holding back and he expects the same response from his disciples.

The great acted parable in John's Gospel, where Jesus takes a towel and a basin and washes his disciples' feet,[7] is intended to convey just such a message. As the nature of God is self-giving so must we expect to act toward each other. Interestingly, Peter finds it very difficult to accept that ministry – a point to which we shall return. Jesus's action indicates to his disciples the nature of God's love and that their response is to be an attitude of loving self-giving, reflecting the attitude of God in Christ to them. It is important also to recognise the other side of this episode – receiving is as much part of loving as giving.[8]

The nature of discipleship is also understood in terms of giving. The disciples are "given the secret of the kingdom of God"; it is not a secret which can somehow be earned or achieved. The givenness of the secret is part of God's plan, so that they may see and hear and perceive and understand when all around them are blind and deaf to the ways of God. This perception and discernment are gifts. To see and understand something of the ways of God is not a natural attribute but a gift from God. It becomes clear later that this gift, as with all gifts given by God, is for the purpose of making known the ways of God to others. That does not mean, however, that the others will necessarily hear. So, giving is at the centre of God's dealing with man. It is not surprising that Jesus ends this section by indicating that giving begets giving, and those who accept the secret and pass it on will themselves receive even more, for they will enter more fully into the secret.[9] Mark follows this saying with two little parables which bear this out. What starts small and apparently insignificant, given the right conditions, grows beyond all imagining.

Another element in Jesus's teaching on giving involves the handing over of authority. The most obvious parables related to this are those of the tenants in the vineyard[10] and the talents.[11] Both of them have as their setting an absentee ruler or owner who, having authority and riches, hands it over to others and goes away for a long time. In each case the question: How do you react to and use that which has been entrusted to you? The tenants try to assume a total but spurious responsibility by refusing to accept that they are under the authority of the owner. Eventually in killing the owner's son they hope to achieve complete ownership for themselves. The result is that they lose what they had and, in the event, their own lives as well. Their heritage will then be given to others. Clearly the parable is aimed at the Jewish authorities. If they act as though they own what God has given them as a gift to use for his purposes, then they will lose all to the Gentiles. A totally unacceptable possibility.

In the parable of the talents[12] each servant is entrusted with money and required to use it. That two of them make more is acceptable for they have taken their authority seriously and recognised that they are responsible to the ruler. The third one is equally responsible in his own eyes – he plays it safe – making sure that the owner receives at least that with which he entrusted this servant. But the owner of the money deals with him harshly. The point is that following Christ is a risky business. If we accept the gifts, we must be prepared to lose them, for the nature of God's gifts are such that they cannot be stored away against a day of reckoning. The reckoning comes when we are made aware of how little we have used the gifts with which God has entrusted us.

The parable of the sheep and the goats[13] deals with the same theme. The basis of the judgment is whether people actually did what they said they had done. The contrast is therefore between those who say they do the will of God, but in practice do not do anything about it, and those whose concern for others is such that they are unaware of how fully they have done the will of God. The parable reflects the logical judgment on the priest and the Levite in the parable of the Good Samaritan. They were quick to make the laws and equally quick to pass by. It took the Samaritan to do the real giving. So with the sheep in the other parable. They have given in all sorts of ways, simply because they are aware of the need, and not for any self-conscious motives. The goats, on the other hand, appear to have done all manner of good works in their own eyes, but have missed the real needs.

Receiving

Perhaps the place to start here is with that delightful incident recorded in all three synoptic Gospels, in which Jesus very

firmly and beautifully puts the disciples in their place.[14] The
context is typical: the disciples have been arguing as to who is
the greatest. It is amazing to me how often I claim to be
following the Lord of Life, and all the time I am so obsessed
with my own greatness and importance, that I cannot even
recognise that one so much greater than me is walking ahead.
I am horrified at how little I really see of Jesus, because of my
pride, my independence and lovelessness. So it is with the
disciples. Walking behind him, they are like little boys boast-
ing of their prowess and their skills. When asked what they
were discussing, they became silent – it was too petty, and
before Jesus, it was irrelevant. Then Jesus put things in
perspective: "and he took a child and put him in the midst of
them; and taking him in his arms, he said to them 'Whoever
receives one such little child in my name, receives me; and
whoever receives me, receives not me, but him who sent
me." Self-importance is deflated when it is able to receive.
Giving when I am self-important only communicates a sense
of patronising graciousness, and that is sin. But sin is rendered
meaningless when we see a lowly creature and are able to see
God in him. Receiving is a wonderful gift, for it sets things in
proportion. True humility is recognising that one is no more
important than a little child, so frequently overlooked. Receiving ensures that we stay dependent.

Let us turn back to Peter, as he refuses to let Jesus wash his
feet. William Temple, commenting on Jesus's action in
washing the disciples' feet, says: "Man's humility does not
begin with the beginning of service; it begins with the readiness to receive it. For there can be much pride and condescen-
sion in our giving of service."[15] Peter's rejection comes surely
from a sense of his own inadequacy – how can the Lord do
this to me? But it is just that sense of inadequacy which has to
be brought under submission. Unless Peter is prepared to
receive the love which God gives, in spite of his feelings of
unworthiness, there is no chance of him being able to partici-
pate with Jesus in his ongoing ministry. What Peter needs to
accept is that though Jesus is Lord, he comes as a slave to

those who do not deserve such treatment. But in the receiving of that ministry, Peter has the chance to enter into a fuller and deeper relationship with Jesus and the other disciples. The horror of unworthiness is no excuse for not accepting the love of God. It is precisely because we are unworthy that the amazing self-giving of God in Jesus comes more clearly into focus.

As Jesus sends out the twelve on their mission, the criterion for ministry which they are to use is whether those to whom they are sent will receive them or not.[16] In receiving them they accept the authority under which the twelve are sent, and in that acceptance, they receive the Kingdom. The point is even more effectively made in the prologue to John's Gospel. "He came to his own home, and his own people received him not. But to all who received him, who believed in his name, he gave the power to become children of God."[17] Again in John's Gospel, it is the receiving of the Holy Spirit which distinguishes those who are of God from those who are of the world.[18] Thus receiving is part of salvation; to receive is to be under authority – the authority of God. That means accepting the responsibility which comes from being under that authority and living out the consequences in a world which refuses to accept it.

Giving and receiving in Jesus's own life

There are two particular incidents in the Gospels which are specially relevant at this point. The first is the story, recounted only in Luke, of the ten lepers.[19] Essentially, it is of a group of lepers, outcast from society, who are healed of their terrible disease and, in the excitement of realising that they are only one step away from readmission to society, hurry off to the priests to have their cure authenticated. Only one, an outcast, a Samaritan, surely more despised than the lepers themselves, is able to receive the healing, and give thanks to Jesus while at the same time glorifying God. Jesus recognises the faith (the constant emphasis of Jesus's teaching is that faith and not birth is the key to entry into the Kingdom) and pronounces a healing greater than the cure of leprosy. Here is a man who, having received, recognises the source of his healing, the authority which conquers the evil, and gives thanks for what he has received. As a result, he is made whole in a way which the others, though cleansed from their leprosy, are not. It is the two-way action of receiving and giving which brings about the true salvation.

The other incident is also related only by Luke. It tells of the woman of the streets, who anoints Jesus with ointment and tears.[20] There is a remarkable double significance here. There is first the contrast between the woman and the somewhat superior and self-righteous Simon – which I take to be the main point of the incident. But the thing for us to concentrate on is how Jesus is prepared to accept her ministrations for her own good. He allows her to "waste" the ointment, he allows her to make what must have felt like a public spectacle of him and he receives her love and the pouring out of her own unworthiness. As she anoints and kisses Jesus, he simply accepts that this is what she has to offer, and he does so lovingly and very sensitively. When Simon complains, he tells the story of the two debtors and then turns back to the woman: "Your faith has saved you; go in peace." So by his acceptance, he gives her salvation and – that most desired of all gifts – peace. She is made whole because Jesus accepts what is essentially an act of worship – of overwhelming self-giving.

The Last Supper has the same ingredients, of breaking and giving in this case.[21] The disciples are enjoined to receive what he gives and, in so doing, a new Covenant is instituted. That this action became the centre of Christian worship very early in the life of the Church, is inevitable. It sums up so much of Jesus's ministry and points us to the supreme symbol of giving and receiving – the Cross.

Before we look again at the Cross, just one or two other points. Jesus seems to have enjoyed people and company – he was accused of being a "glutton and a drunkard",[22] presumably because he accepted hospitality and enjoyed a party! Certainly he accepted hospitality from Simon the leper, which we have just seen; from Zacchaeus,[23] and from Martha and Mary;[24] to say nothing of many undisclosed hosts. The fascinating thing is that, as Jesus accepts their love and hospitality, or even a rather grudging invitation from Simon, he nevertheless in the receiving seems to make it possible for others to come to a new awareness of themselves and a new life – salvation. That is very important for the counselling process.

So to the Cross again! We cannot go far without being aware of what it means for our salvation. Think of what Jesus receives – anger, hatred, deception, jealousy, indifference, mob violence, organised brutality, mockery and just plain cruelty – to say nothing of the darkness of the whole history of human sin, which envelops him and his moment of agony and fear. All of that amounts to an acceptance of the will of the Father and the preparedness to be obedient, even when he could see no way through the hell of his situation. And what he gives is a gentleness, a silence, a declaration of who he is, a dignity, a care for others, and a concern for his mother. He requests forgiveness for his executioners, gives insight into his agony of soul and, at his death, a glimpse past the curtain of the Holy of Holies, to the very nature of God himself.

Yes, the Cross involves a receiving and a giving; receiving all the sin that man can pour out on to him; and giving LIFE in return – new life, abounding life bursting from sin and fear to a declaration of freedom, God's greatest gift to man. That is the resource of the Christian, the minister, the counsellor, any who call on his name.

Giving and receiving in counselling

Probably the most difficult thing in counselling is for the counsellee to *accept that he needs help in the first place*. Our pride tells us we ought to be able to cope on our own, and sin tells us we are to be *in*dependent. It is rather like the prodigal son – a time comes when the problem outweighs the pride and dependence seems at least slightly preferable to in-dependence.

Having come that far, there is the question of trust. If we go to someone, will we be able to trust him? Will we be able to confide with confidence? Will he understand our problems? These are critical questions for they are essential if there is to be an adequate counselling relationship.

There are other problems as well. It is most unusual for a husband to successfully counsel his wife or vice versa; or a parent a child. Very frequently that is where we will turn first; for that is where we feel safest – but we are not. The emotion-al relationship between the members of the family is almost certainly tied up with the problem. The counsellor in that context would become part of the problem, and there is little help to be gained from that quarter. Often relationships have to be repaired in precisely those areas and the counsellee needs someone who can stand outside the problems.

All of this is part of the background to giving and receiving. Essentially what we must realise is that the counsellor does not give because it is his task but because he loves the person with the love of Christ. Easily said, but not easily done. I know some who counsel because they want to be needed. That may be fine up to a point, but they will have difficulty breaking off the relationship. I know others who counsel because they are "good at it". That may be all right too, but it will become self-centred. I know others who go through the motions because it is expected of them – that is awful and they should not do it. I know all of these very well because I have been them myself. And so I know without any doubt that the only adequate motive for counselling is that at that moment one represents Christ, in all his love, to the counsellee.

Empathy and compassion

Almost every book on counselling I have come across emphasises the need for empathy rather than sympathy. That I can understand, for sympathy says something like "I feel so sorry for you", which does not really help the person to deal with the problem. Empathy on the other hand, gets inside the feelings and shows that the feelings are both understandable and acceptable and also that there is a way out of them.

One of my first experiences of bereavement was a very tragic experience on board a ship. I had been studying in England and, newly ordained and very raw, I was still getting used to my clerical collar. About five days out from Cape Town, I was summoned by the captain (it was a large passenger liner) and asked to do a funeral and "look after the old man's daughter". I did the funeral and went to see the daughter, who was in a terrible state. In eighteen months she had lost her mother and her brother, and had been to England to collect her father for him to live with her and her family in South Africa. Now he, too, was dead and she was badly shattered. I spent the whole afternoon with her and instinctively (it could not have been anything else, because nobody had trained me how to deal with bereavement, in spite of my clerical collar) I asked questions about her family and encouraged her to talk about them. Gradually the grief gave way to an enjoyment of the good times and good qualities and when I left her, she was at peace and wanted to have an early night. Next morning I went to her cabin to find it filled with four or five very sympathetic women sitting round her, all relating how their relatives had died and the poor woman was in a worse condition than before. It was clear the women were doing their duty, but the sympathy was not enough and all they had done was make matters worse. Sympathy can be a very debilitating response because, while it is concerned, it does not really take the other person's feelings seriously. Empathy on the other hand identifies with the feelings and accepts them as real and accepts the person as genuine in the process. It communicates that acceptance.

Jesus is not, however, described in terms which entirely fit the definitions of empathy. It was a former student of mine who came visiting a while ago and had seen most clearly that empathy is only part of the answer. Jesus brings another dimension – compassion. That involves more than feeling with, rather it understands at the deepest level of need and agonises with. Jesus's compassion allows the woman to make a fool of herself and him in public – and it brings her peace. Jesus's compassion is described by Mark in terms of a rending of the bowels – an agony of involvement, which affects the deepest seat of the feelings.[25] So in the agony of that love, the leper is cleansed. Jesus is not an uninvolved saviour; on the contrary, the reason why he is able to be so effective is that he is so deeply involved.

So, the Christian counsellor is to exercise compassion and that will mean a depth of giving and receiving which we can never fully fathom. Giving and receiving have all sorts of consequences in the counselling process. For the counsellor to receive, means that he can share in some sense the freedom of being dependent on God and on others. He will receive and accept the feelings of the counsellee, he will accept that he is not able to see or discern all, he will accept his own inadequacies and lack of insight and he will accept the power of the Spirit, which makes him open to the other person. He will give of his awareness of the presence of God, he will share his compassion, his knowledge, both formal and experiential, his caring, without taking sides or assuming that what the counsellee is saying is the only truth. He will cut through to the centre of the matter, with a gentleness and firmness which allows for growth, because in the process it removes the deadness and cleans out the emotional wounds. He will exercise an overwhelming love, which is at the heart of the Cross.

Equally, he will allow the person to become dependent on him if necessary – for a while – making sure that he transfers the dependence to our Lord as part of the healing. He receives the hatred and anger of the other person's feelings and, in compassion, comes closer to Christ, who alone helps both counsellor and client to the insights necessary to true wholeness. His concern is the counsellee. He does not worry about himself. He will not allow himself to get in the way. It is one thing to allow a temporary dependency as a bridge to Christ, but he must never allow himself to be a barrier between the client and the one or ones to whom he should be reconciled. It is the counsellor's task to open those gates. It is a risky business at times, so the counsellor has to have a very clear vision of where he is going and not be diverted from it. It is one thing not to know the next step and to pray for discernment and guidance, it is another to have lost the way and not know what to aim for. The aim is always the same: a wholeness of the person as he comes to a living experience of our Lord. And at that point, we will be like the Baptist:

> You yourselves bear me witness, that I said, I am not the Christ, but I have been sent before him. He who has the bride is the bridegroom; the friend of the bridegroom, who stands and hears him, rejoices greatly at the bridegroom's voice. Therefore this joy of mine is now full. He must increase and I must decrease.[26]

We will not be important, because Christ will be all in all.

One last point: giving and receiving implies freedom – a freedom to follow Jesus, even when the world disapproves and social convention says something else. It is a freedom to know Jesus and serve him, a freedom to be the servant of all and the slave of Christ.

Chapter
9

The Love of God in Counselling

We saw in the previous chapter that the essence of love is giving and receiving – or should it be the other way around? We must now try to draw together some insights relating to love and acceptance by looking at what Jesus taught on the subject and seeing how he lived it. It will be illuminating for the counselling process.

Perhaps the most often repeated truism is that everybody needs love and acceptance. All the books on counselling, whether Christian or not, aim at helping a person to a degree of self-acceptance. That would include acceptance of others, an ability to live with themselves, an ability to live with problems. Almost every problem has at its heart some degree of lovelessness. No matter how it is described, no matter how it is experienced, lovelessness hurts, for it is the core of sin. Sin destroys love and puts in its place an illusion of power, and a worse illusion that we alone can decide what is right for us. That is loveless – and the tragedy is that most people are unaware of the condition.

My family was discussing wealth the other day. I had heard of a professional man who was earning in the region of £100,000 per annum. Even allowing for taxation and overheads, that is still an enormous amount of money; more so in a country where the majority of people earn less than one hundredth of that in a year. We were asking ourselves what can one *do* with money like that? Well, we can live in a luxury house – probably too big for one's needs; we can buy a bigger and better car; educate our children more expensively; buy a yacht, clothes, furniture and anything else that takes one's fancy. That may be true; we could even go overseas every year or so; but in the end, would we be any better off? We might eat the finest food, have an army of servants, but would we be more considerate, loving, selfless? Would our relationships be better? I sometimes think that the marriages of people who have too much may easily end up as hollow shells – packed around with things, but with no foundation of loving selflessness.

I asked a young couple recently if they found that sleeping together actually expressed their love outside the commitment of marriage. Sex is no substitute for love and while they honestly believed that it *had* brought them closer, I am sure that that path is fraught with difficulties. Sex is not love. Sex should be the physical expression of a loving relationship which is based on strong elements of friendship and simple companionship. Then the means of procreation becomes a glorious act of sheer self-giving. To use sex as a short cut in a relationship is not loving, it is selfish and leads to selfishness. Human loving is so often inadequate, grasping what it can get.

At the centre of the Christian faith is the Cross. It symbolises the love of a God who would rather die than force people to follow him. Yet it is not an undirected thing; it points to his way for living. It leads by promising new life if we are prepared to abandon the old; it attacks sin and dies for the sinner; it overcomes the selfishness of men by the selflessness of him who gave himself for us. There are no short cuts, nor are there easy answers. The love of God is so simple that men either look past it or balk at it; its very simplicity demands a selfless response with no reward other than the loving itself. The love of God is a self-sacrificing love which absorbs sin without compromising its position. The love of God is a reality in history, giving rise to the Church, the community which exists to embody the love of God and to live by it. There is of course a vast chasm between the ideals which the Church enshrines and the reality of her actions. No one who knows anything about Church history will want to defend a view which suggests that the Church has consistently and devotedly lived out the love of God. But, strangely, the Church, with all its faults and imperfections, its divisions and arrogance, still proclaims and exists to live out the reality of God's love amidst men and nations. The Church, deformed body that it may be, still makes known the impossible: that God's love is a reality by which people may live, and for which they may die. In the process God is proclaimed, his glory revealed and people saved.

The love of God is not a sentimental amorphous thing. It focuses on Jesus, a man with a history and a vision of God. His claims of Messiahship are important, but it is his calling of all men to trust him which gives him a universality and clarity frequently missed by us who see through sin-sick eyes. He comes to judge, not by damning, but by showing us ourselves as we were intended to be. He reveals the love of God which man rejects. For those who accept him "He gave power to become children of God".[1] Men want power, but go to great lengths to have it on their terms. That is not God's way. God shows us a different style of living. "God so loved that he gave his only son."[2] Man's love is different. If he loves something he snatches "it". "I love you – I want you." "I love that thing, I want it." God's love is in direct contrast to the sort of power-grabbing love we are used to.

Jesus's teaching on love

The obvious place to start is with the Sermon on the Mount. Here, as we face Jesus, we see a set of values which bowls us over and yet gives us hope. The teaching of the Sermon has been described by C. J. Langenhoven, a South African who wrote in Afrikaans, as a series of "shocking paradoxes".[3] Shocking or not, they face us with radical insights, into man's relationships as a result of God's involvement with him, and into the nature of the love of God himself.

Jesus turns the values of the world upside down, and gives a new dimension to life and living. The question is why? The answer lies in the nature of God. Inevitably, Jesus the Jew would have taken the Old Testament insights into God for granted. He knew of the great act at Sinai, where the Israelites are set aside to make known the presence of God to the nations. He knew of the holiness of God and his justice and righteousness. But he also knew that everything which Israel stood for was only a pale reflection of the aweful majesty of God the Creator and King who demands obedience and commitment yet gives a relationship with himself and others which sets them apart as recognisably his people, holy and elect. All of that of course means a different way of living and for the people of the Old Testament, that was summed up in the "Shema" – "Hear O Israel: The Lord our God is one Lord; and you shall love the Lord your God with all your heart and with all your soul and with all your might."[4]

The Levitical injunction,[5] which is quoted to Jesus by the scribe, is only a small part of a chapter which sets out what it means for the people of Israel to be holy. The motive is quite straightforward – "for I the Lord your God am holy". Thus "revering" parents is one aspect – giving them the loving respect which comes from recognising your dependence upon them. Keeping Sabbath, honesty, the way you farm and carry on your business, all of these constitute a different way of living. Oppression, injustice, partiality in the law, slander, hatred, are all to be rooted out; there is no place for them in the holy people of God. And then at last, by contrast to the negative values which have been set out in some detail, we read: "You shall not take vengeance or bear any grudge against the sons of your own people, but you shall *love your neighbour as yourself: I am the Lord.*"[6] So when Jesus gives us an ethic which in many ways goes beyond what Judaism required, he does so out of an intimate awareness of the nature of Abba – of God himself. Von Rad suggests that here "stress is laid on love for God as the only feeling worthy of God",[7] so too is the response of loving one's neighbour.

Jesus does not often teach directly about the nature of God, but much of what he says implies it. At the heart of God is a self-giving love which desires that the whole of creation should live by that same love. It is that which produces peace, and that which produces the desire for the best for each other. God's love knows no bounds, so that the smallest particles of life, a hair, a sparrow, an insignificant lost person who has strayed from God, a revoltingly wounded half dead traveller, are all desperately important. So too are the offscourings of humanity with whom he gladly consorts and eats. At the heart of God is an overwhelming compassion, and that is reflected repeatedly in Jesus's teaching. Forgiveness, kindness, joy are all manifestations of his love. The other man's need is an unrepeatable opportunity. Love is not simply approval of the other person, or being kind to those you like, it involves being kind and loving to the very one trying to kill you. That sort of attitude is life-changing; it humanises in such a way that people see past "the enemy" to a person beloved by God. *Miracle on the River Kwai* by Ernest Gordon[8] bears eloquent testimony, if testimony is needed, to that sort of living. It is a matter of fact that God's love is the only truly revolutionary force in history, and the most difficult to accept. Leviticus makes it clear that every aspect of life comes under the liberating authority of the Lord of Creation. That alone humanises and gives meaning to life.

The love of God also, and inevitably, involves judgment. Many is the person who wants to accept the love of God, but is unhappy to look at the element of judgment which is integral to love. The point is simple and necessary. Judgment is that aspect of God's involvement with man which exposes man's sinfulness. Absolute love, by its very act of loving, exposes our sin, and Adam and Eve, like we, scamper back into the undergrowth, hoping that the love remains and judgment will not take place. What we do is more than a scampering. Francis Thompson, in his glorious and disturbing poem "The Hound of Heaven", describes it better as a fleeing and the first section sums up man's desperate fear of God's overwhelming love.

I fled Him, down the nights and down the days
I fled Him down the arches of the years;
I fled Him down the labyrinthine ways
Of my own mind; and in the mist of tears
I hid from Him.

No it is not a scampering. It is mad panic-stricken flight. The god of perfection is fearsome to those who are wilful and rebellious.

The judgment of God therefore involves both the trust of man and his demand for obedience. The parables sum up these two elements well. The God-figure of the father in the prodigal son is of one whose love swamps the wilfulness of the wayward son.[9] The ruler who leaves his property to others while he goes off for a lengthy period is exercising another element of love – trust. The fact that the tenants are untrustworthy means that they must accept the inevitable judgment implicit in attempting to take what is not theirs.[10] So, too, the master of the servants to whom he left money.[11] In each case the master trusts – and the underlings are untrustworthy. Judgment must follow for, like it or not, God is not one who condones evil or dishonesty. It is contrary to his nature. The point is that in each of these parables the dominant figure – the ruler or master – is in some way representing the consistency of a loving, trusting, compassionate God. The very fact that God does so love and trust makes it possible for man to be dishonest, to break trust, to go his own way. There is no escape; when the right response is not forthcoming, there must be both punishment and reparation before the relationship can be restored once more. Matthew is rather more dramatic than Luke. Luke keeps the parables on a this-worldly plane; Matthew has a Heaven and hell element which gives the punishment a place in eternity. This is particularly true of that body of parables specifically aimed at judgment.[12] In each case however the primary point of the parable is the loving intent of the king, bridegroom, the man on the long journey, or the King who judges the nations.

In John's Gospel the elements of the love and judgment are more closely drawn. The cleansing of the Temple[13] is put at the beginning of the Gospel precisely to make it known that when the new breaks in, the old has not only to be reformed, but is essentially judged and found wanting. Jesus's words to Nicodemus culminating in the best known of all biblical texts, "For God so loved the world that he gave his only Son, that whoever believes in him should not perish but have eternal life", emphasises that the love of God is given so that there might be faith which leads to a reprieve from eternal death.[14] John spells it out specifically: "This is the judgment, that the light has come into the world, and men loved darkness more than light, because their deeds are evil."[15] There is love here, but it is neither love for God or the love of God. The darkness is more attractive; the judgment is that those who love darkness more than the light (Christ) will simply live on in the darkness and take the consequences of living in evil.

One of the problems for many counsellors whose task it is to help people from darkness to light, is that in the western world at least, belief in evil, either as a corporate or individual force, is often rejected. No matter how converted we are, there are still many areas in our lives where darkness reigns supreme, and if we don't believe it, look at the way we treat or would like to treat our fellow Christians, to say nothing of our fellow humans.

The love of God is more explicitly described further on in John.[16] It is the active, life-giving force of God, pulled by its very nature against the forces of sin, hatred and evil. "He who hates me, hates my Father also . . . but now they have seen and hated both me and my Father."[17] The ultimate aim of the love of God is summed up in Jesus's so called "High priestly prayer"; "I do not pray that thou shouldst take them out of the world, but that thou shouldst keep them from the evil one . . . Sanctify them in the truth; thy word is truth. As thou didst send me into the world, so I have sent them into the world."[18] The love of God is therefore explicit. It protects, certainly, but it is also active and outgoing, for it gives his followers the identity they need to go into the world and win it back for God. That is the purpose of the Gospel.

Again a comment. Frequently the love of God is taught or portrayed as something in which we wallow and enjoy ourselves to no consequence. Jesus did not so teach it. For him, it is active and dynamic, outgoing and outpouring, judging and supporting, giving new life and, most important of all, *new identity*. There is no point in the love of God invading fallen Creation if, in the process, things remain as they are. The love of God is the essential quality of God, expressing his holiness. It is that element which distinguishes him from all else in creation, and distinguishes his followers in the same way. So much of the teaching about the nature of the Church has that element of the love of God as central to it. The Church is the community which seeks to embody the love of God, not because we can do it in our own strength, but because it is his gift to us, to preserve and disseminate.

If the teaching of Jesus concerning the love of God is unequivocal, so are his actions, which keep us pointed to that love. The obvious one is the Cross, but before looking at that, let us notice one or two other aspects of Jesus's life. A good place to start is at the beginning – the Nativity. The love of God cuts across convention and calls people to risk. Mary must have had a wonderful sense of fulfilment at the Annunciation, but the consequences, even though she was married to a good man like Joseph, were scarcely acceptable in society. And Joseph, too, had to bear a considerable doubt.[19] The anger and fear of a king and life in exile, are only part of what God's love means in practice.[20] It is not just the supernatural signs which are important, but the desperate plight of a couple severed from home and living in a foreign land, all because of the love of God. "God so loved that He gave" . . . yes, but for those who follow and have the right to become the sons of God there is no automatic or obvious peace and tranquillity. For Mary there was a sword, turbulence and pain throughout her life. For Joseph, there was doubt and exile, for a while at least. For Jesus, there was the way of temptation

and rejection. The love of God flies in the face of the
world – "and men loved darkness rather than light". Jesus *is*
the love of God and only later were people able to recognise
quite what that meant. So, much later, John can write to
Christian converts and tell them with excitement, "There is
no fear in love, but perfect love casts out fear."[21] For us to get
to that point, we must recognise that the love of God takes us
directly into the areas of fear, there to face the ultimate fear
and know that in him there is life. So death *has* lost its sting,
but that does not make life easy. We may no longer fear death
(and I wonder of how many that is true), but we must now face
life. That is not something snug and comfortable, in which
ostrich-like we may avoid the things that hurt or induce fear.
Facing the things we fear we now know that, in the love of
God, the victory has been won.

The Cross

As we turn to the Cross we start with a declaration from Paul,
of such power that it still resounds through history: "Far be it
from me to glory except in the Cross of Christ"[22] and that has
come to us in the famous hymn which opens: "In the cross of
Christ I glory / Towering o'er the wrecks of time." Strange,
the Cross of Christ, to Jews a scandal and to Greeks stupidity,
is more than anything else the sign of the love of God in the
world.

From Paul's perspective, it is right to talk of the Cross as
triumph. From his view, the grave is a bed of hope, death has
lost its sting. To Jesus it was fear, loneliness and agony; to the
disciples it was terror, confusion and the disintegration of all
their hopes and aspirations. We can so easily sentimentalise
the Cross, unless we see it as God's answer to man's sin. It is
not just a beautifully heroic act; nor is it simply injustice on an
innocent man. It is not folly, nor a scandal, though if it is seen
thus, then at least there is some hope of a response to it. In the
first two interpretations, we have got it all wrong. Paul puts it
well in Romans when he declares: "But God shows his love

for us in that while we were yet sinners Christ died for us."[23]
Love is the God-ingredient for defeating sin, and supremely it
is seen on the Cross.

Mark's Gospel shows that repeatedly. After the declaration of Jesus as Messiah[24] there are three predictions of the
Passion.[25] For Mark these are crucial; hammerblows in his
theological presentation of the saving reality of the God who
loves. The importance of these three predictions lies firstly in
their positions – in each case they come at a point of crisis
(after the declaration of Jesus as Messiah; after the transfiguration and the episode with the epileptic boy; on the road
as they near Jerusalem, with some very difficult teaching on
the cost of following him). They are also important because of
the wording. We need not argue here whether they have been
embellished by the fact that Mark knew the end before he
ever wrote the Gospel. What is significant is the emphatic way
in which the passion is presented. It is not just chance. "The
Son of man must suffer and be rejected."[26] "The Son of man
will be delivered into the hands of men and they will kill
him."[27] "The Son of man will be delivered . . ."[28] It is
scarcely surprising that James and John wanted to know what
was in it for them! There is nothing coincidental about Jesus's
death. It is God's strategy for redemption.

The pattern of death and life is central to the love of God.
Death is more than a physical thing. It involves every emotion
in the range of human feelings. Jesus faces loneliness, fear,
doubt, despair, helplessness, physical pain and the awful
agony of godforsakenness. He faces them and he wins. That is
the message of the Gospel. *Nothing* that the human condition
can produce is powerful enough to overcome the love of God.
God's answer is straightforward and direct. He absorbs the
sin of the universe with all its byproducts, and keeps on
loving. So, far from being sentimental and weak, it is strong
and devastating, it breaks the forces which bind and gives to
man the one thing he needs more than anything else – hope.

Hope is the most powerful ingredient in the counselling
situation. Give a person hope and he has new life. So many

counselling procedures, while claiming hope, seem in reality to substitute one form of bondage for another, creating the wrong type of dependencies. The love of God creates the only true relationship – dependence on him alone. That is the counsellor's purpose. The Anglican Collect for Morning Prayer sums it up well when it declares that the service of God "is perfect freedom".

Before we move on and see how all this applies to the counselling process, it may be useful to look at the wide range of the word "love" and remind ourselves of its meaning. The obvious beginning, and certainly the one with which the world is obsessed, is sexual love. It is the expression of the natural attractions between man and woman. Sexual attractions are always with us and for many, sex seems the only adequate expression of any relationship. It is not. At the best, it is the physical sign of a relationship already in existence. At the worst, it degenerates into lust; a temporary satisfaction of physical and emotional selfishness.

Closely related to sexual love is brotherly love, or, as I have called it elsewhere, friendship. This is a delightful love – close, warm, supportive and accepting. Friendship is what most of us need most of the time. Affection and companionship are the hallmarks of it. Openness and fearlessness are very much part of it. An ability to accept criticism is integral to it, for the love counterbalances the fear of rejection which so often threatens in criticism.

When both sexual love and friendship combine, one has the perfect ingredients for marriage, so married love is another type of love. This has the dimension of permanence and commitment in any situation, "for better for worse, for richer for poorer, in sickness and in health, till death us do part". The family is a logical conclusion to married love. Most couples see children as essential to their expectations of marriage.

Finally there is the love of God – love which sacrifices itself for others. The Greek *agape* has an overwhelming sense of giving, of caring for the other person, of loving others at least as much as we love ourselves. It is in this category that self-love or self-acceptance comes, for it recognises the wonder of a life given by God to be used in his service.

While the first three loves might be seen as the best forms of human response, *agape* is the love which only God can give. We see it most clearly on the Cross. The love of God is the cement which binds all the other loves. We cannot do without love. If we do not have an outlet for sexual love, we can survive. It must then be channelled into some other aspect of living, there to express itself in some other form of self-giving. Promiscuity is no substitute for love, it is a terrible dead end, where none of the other loves may be adequately lived out. We also need friendship, we cannot do without it. Man was made as a creature of community. To be with people who accept us is to delight in a fulfilment which is of God. Not all are called to marriage, but all are called to express themselves in community. If God has not called us to establish a family with a partner in marriage, then he may be calling us to express ourselves in other relationships which are no less creative and fulfilling. Yet none of these loves has final meaning, unless it is drawn beyond the immediate, to the ultimate of God. God is love, so all love is taken up into him. As he loves us, so in truth, we are able to love others. "Perfect love casts out fear"; there is the wonder of God – a love where selfishness (which is surely only another element in fear) is taken up into the eternal dimensions of a loving God.

God's love in counselling

Most people who come for counselling have a problem of identity. That is not only true of people who come for counselling, all of us have it to some extent. I do not consider myself more than averagely maladjusted, but I find it very difficult to accept that I am a son of God or that I am beloved of others. Even when I am continually reassured I have the greatest difficulty in trusting those assurances. Within me is a deep-rooted feeling of not knowing who I am, and not liking

what little I do know. At times that has become so much of a
problem that I have had to seek help from a counsellor. The
problem is quite simple. If I cannot trust God or man, I cannot
trust myself – and if I trust myself, then I cannot possibly live
out the faith and the life given me by God. It is only as I am
helped to experience the love of God and accept that he loves
me now, and always has, that I can rest assured in an identity
which I do not have to prove, or worry about.

So in practice the love of God means that every aspect of
life is under the rule and dynamic care of God. The God who
loves, creates. As creator, nothing is too small or insignificant. Many will say that they "do not want to worry God
with little things". That somehow implies a very human God
with a scale of priorities. But the love of God declares that
every thing in life comes under his care and, as such, its
meaning and importance can only be found in him. For many
people that is the point of release and growth: to discover,
with awe, that we are confronted with a God who takes all of
experience seriously. That means all experience is under his
judgment. Judgment then is either frightening or liberating.
Either we do not want God involved (in which case we
continue to love darkness rather than light) or else we will
want to walk in the light. The acceptance of the pain and joy
of judgment are then the ways in which God gives direction
and keeps us in the light. So identity is his gift to us. To help
people *know* the love of God, and *know* that in his love they
have a meaning, is a priority for the counsellor. That is more
easily said than achieved. It is a process where the pains of
rejection and the bewilderment of lostness give way to the
awareness that in the whole of creation I am unique, beloved
and have a purpose. It means facing the lostness and daring to
look beyond to a new life.

The love of God also brings judgment. Many people think
of judgment in terms of a vindictive God, who enjoys seeing
those whom he has created toasted perpetually on the end of a
devilish fork. That is not the God of the Bible. Nor is
judgment seen exclusively in terms of a court room, although

that image is very much part of the prophets and apocalyptic writing and certainly has a place in the teaching of Jesus. The biblical vision of judgment is of a God who loves us so much that he dies for us and who, in his love, shows us how far short of his image we have fallen. The ultimate condemnation is to be totally outside the ambit of God. If we are there, then we will indeed weep and gnash our teeth, not because that is where we have been consigned, but because outside the influence and love of God, we are nothing. That is eternal torment; it is also what people fear most.

Judgment is being confronted with the perfect love of God and recognising it for what it is. That is a devastating experience, but it is also, surprisingly, life-giving. For it gives hope in a situation where many people are hopeless. It breaks the awful bondage of a life lived to no other purpose than doing my own dreary will. For many, the judgment of God is a moment of pure liberation and life.

There is another element to it however. For many, the judgment of God comes because they are deliberately and wilfully disobedient. The person who neglects his family has eventually to face judgment. How he accepts that will determine life or death for him and the family.

As a student at university, I went away on a rugby trip and quite deliberately and cold-bloodedly got drunk. The university was small, news travelled fast. The incident caused a scandal and dismay amongst the Christians on the campus. Rightly so. The following evening a person whom I had never liked, who was also studying for the ministry, came to my room and said that my action was disgraceful and that I had betrayed both God and his Church. He went on to say that he would not leave my room until I had repented. The truth of the matter was that I was feeling disgusted with myself, but my pride refused to say anything to the person I disliked so much. He stayed; I gave in, and experienced probably for the first time in my life, the overwhelming sense of forgiveness and love in contrast to the terrible wilfulness of my sin. Over the years I have still not learnt to like that particular person very much. He is a very good priest in South Africa, and though I thank God for him, I am not sure we have very much in common. I tell this story for it has a number of points worth noting.

The first is that my action required what Howard Clinebell describes as "Confrontational Counselling".[29] For nothing else would have got me out of the cocoon of defiance and self-justification ("I can lead my own life – who are they to tell me what to do?"). Equally, Ted did not sit in judgment. He did not communicate that he was better than me – he simply told me that I had fallen short of the behaviour required of a follower of Christ. He also did not let me off the hook, he was not going to let me get away with my own behaviour. So repentance and forgiveness brought for me an awareness of the presence of God in my life that I had never known before. Thank God for Ted.

The counselling ministry involves helping people to the love of God, a love which burns dross as it refines the life. The counsellor must be aware of that, and aware that he, too, is under the same judgment. The other great joy in counselling is to see people grow in trust – trust of God, of self, of others. This, too, comes when we become aware that the love of God gives our lives a direction and purpose. It is essential to realise that all human loves are grounded in him. So we need love, the loves of men and the love of God together in order to find the harmony and balance of life together. Often counselling involves trying to help a person to move away from or even to give up one aspect of human love, so that he can find the others. Obsession with sex will cut out friendship. Obsession with family can cut out other friendships. Over-involvement in any of them means that they are not able to recognise or accept the love of God.

Earlier in this chapter I quoted from Francis Thompson's "The Hound of Heaven". I want to close with the last few lines – they say it all and say it better than I. The writer has finally stopped running and he is awaiting the awful judgment of God. God is speaking (the italics are mine).

"Whom wilt thou find to love ignoble thee
Save Me, save only Me?
All that which I took from thee I did but take,
Not for thy harms,
But just that *thou mightst seek it in My arms*.
All which thy child's mistake
Fancies as lost, I have stored for thee at home:
Rise, clasp My hand, and come!"

Halts by me that footfall
Is my gloom, after all
Shade of His hand, outstretched caressingly?
"Ah, fondest, blindest, weakest,
I am He whom thou seekest!
Thou drawest love from thee, who drawest Me."

Chapter
10

Models

I have called this chapter "Models" because I want to look at the different ways in which Jesus deals with people. Sometimes it seems as though he uses a variety of methods with the same person and, certainly, he has an unerring ability to say the thing which helps people to see with life changing clarity. In seeing, they are open to the power of God mediated through our Lord. As far as I am concerned, there can be no other purpose in counselling; to help a person see himself and see Jesus so that he may experience the healing presence of the Saviour, and in the process take the first steps which lead to salvation.

One of the reasons for writing this book is the need to disagree with what I believe to be two major areas of error frequently found in books on counselling. The first is an insistence that it must be done "this way only". That counselling is a process which can be learnt, step by step, from a book and that people will fit into neatly defined boxes. Often the writer will have much of value to say but the rigidity of the framework denies a person his unique individuality and contrasts sharply with the Gospels' witness to the fact that Jesus is remarkably open and adaptable in his dealings with people.

The second is much more prevalent and just as bothersome. It involves an attitude to counselling which sets its goals no higher than the counsellee himself; helping the person to come to grips with himself, understand himself, accept himself, help himself; so that he may relate better to himself and others. It is a predominantly humanistic approach, which allows no real place for the loving, involved God. I have, for example, learned a great deal over many years from Howard Clinebell, and his incredibly helpful book *Basic Types of Pastoral Counselling*[1] is one which I put into the hands of my students. It is wise and balanced and, having heard Clinebell lecture, I am sure he is a man who knows and loves the Lord. But pastoral counselling as presented by him seems to be a process where God, at the best, plays a very limited role; where the insights of psychology are somehow more important than the dynamic of the God of creation. There is one slightly extended discussion of the Christian perspective in counselling[2] and several passing references, but he is so absorbed in the person, that he forgets – it seems to me – the Saviour. Writing as he does in 1966 (I am aware that the book has been revised since then but I have not seen the revision), he presupposes the reactions against God and traditional God language, which seems to make him avoid mentioning the saving power of the loving God. But he does not put anything in its place. The psychological and secular counselling insights reign supreme.

The issue, therefore, is not that the writers on counselling are incompetent – far from it – but that they only seem to go a part of the way; they stop short of the difference which God makes as he, too, through the power of the Spirit, is an active partner in the counselling process. It would appear that the insights of psychology and the writings on counselling have taken such a grip, that the Christian counsellors have lost their nerve and believe that nothing other than that written in the non-Christian fields can have any real validity. That, of course, is nonsense. We have available to us the power of the spirit of God, which directs and guides, and we have the models which Jesus gives us, in his own relationships with others.

As important, we are inheritors of the great legacy of spiritual and emotional insight through the ages and this, too, focuses on Jesus as he interacts with others. All the great writers on the spiritual life, having soaked themselves in the words and actions of Jesus, are deft in helping people to see themselves as Christ would have them see. So the Christian counsellor has no need to be ashamed of his heritage. In many ways, he is saying very similar things to the secular counsellor. In many areas he is able to throw light on attitudes and situations to which the secular counsellor cannot get close. We have no cause for arrogance in that situation, only confidence that if we keep our eyes on him, we will not go far wrong.

When I worked on a part-time basis in a mental institution, I found myself used by the medical and nursing staff, not because I was excellent at psychiatry, or had great psychological insights; rather, because I approached people in a different way. As a result, the medical staff would ask me to give an opinion on, or to attempt to help a patient, because they felt they were unable to get through to him or her themselves. I had only a theological and ministerial training, but I gained acceptance by trying to be helpful, seeing myself as part of a God-ordained team, whose variety of insights and background was to be used for the health and growth of the patients. Those were wonderful days, because they proved to me that we as Christian counsellors have as much to say in those situations as anyone else, provided we do not think that we can or must say everything!

So let us turn now to some of the models which Jesus gives us for our counselling.

1. Nicodemus[3]

Nicodemus is a fairly common type. He is attracted to Jesus, but he has his position to uphold. He does not want to be seen consorting with Jesus and yet, clearly, he is one who wants more than his own studies and insights have brought him. He recognises something in Jesus, but is sufficiently fearful of losing face, that he must perforce come secretly. He is an "intellectual", a man learned in the Law and in the ways of Judaism, yet one who is humble enough to want to learn more. He got more than he anticipated!

Jesus does not try to carry the argument to Nicodemus on his own terms. He starts by going far beyond the insights and learning of Nicodemus. He turns him to a dimension of Judaism which was clearly not discussed. He links being "born again" with a knowledge of the Kingdom of God.[4] The problem is that born again, and the obvious later reference to baptism are quite beyond the area in which Nicodemus feels secure. He tries taking what Jesus says literally, but that will not do. Jesus shows to Nicodemus aspects of his faith of which he is unaware[5] and takes him further than he expects. But Jesus not only talks in obscurities, he points Nicodemus to a new dimension of his own faith and a new way of seeing Jesus, God and himself. Jesus begins by startling Nicodemus; he ends by challenging him. Essentially, he asks, "Do you prefer darkness rather than light?" and then pushes it further: "are you so ashamed of me that you prefer darkness to light?" In other words, will Nicodemus's action of coming to Jesus in the night continue, or will Nicodemus see past Jesus the social embarrassment to Jesus the Son of God? It is good, therefore, to see Nicodemus defending Jesus in the Council;[6] and at his burial Nicodemus is described as having "at first come to him by night",[7] indicating surely that Nicodemus had later been openly consorting with Jesus – walking in the light.

So the pattern is clear. Jesus starts where Nicodemus is, takes him away from the purely intellectual to a new vision of the faith he knows so well. From that he leads him to an awareness of the love of God and a surprising courage. Jesus is the difference in Nicodemus's life and that is the factor which plunges him into new life.

2. The woman taken in adultery[8]

In many ways this is one of the most attractive of the incidents reported about Jesus. The fact that the manuscripts do not know where to put it, does not mean that it is not authentic. It has all the marks of being as genuine as any other incident in the Gospel and has much to tell us about relationships.

The story is simple. Within a context of teaching in the Temple, surrounded by many people, Jesus is about to be tricked. Clearly the Law declares that adultery is punishable by death. This spurious Rabbi will have his work cut out to make anything else out of a clear-cut case of adultery. It almost seems as though they are on their way to stone her, when they seek to discredit him in the eyes of the people. So Jesus has a double problem: a case of a human being who has clearly sinned in a way which, if allowed to go unchecked, could lead to the moral disintegration of society and cold-hearted men who want her death and him discredited. Jesus deals with them separately. He helps the custodians of Law and nation see that the stones they are about to throw could as well be thrown at them. It would appear that they learnt the lesson reluctantly – ashamed, perhaps, at their own harshness and desire to score off him.

The woman is treated differently. Jesus has no need to condemn her – the Law has already done that. The difference is that now there is no one to carry out the sentence and Jesus has no intention of doing so. Jesus recognises her need for love and acceptance, but does not condone her action. His injunction to "go and do not sin again" makes it clear that he has recognised the sin and forgiven the sinner. She is not simply let off with a caution, rather she is to lead a life strictly within the confines of the Law. Again, the difference in that situation as opposed to countless others before and since, is Jesus. He stands as Judge of *all* sin, and all sin is to be seen in the light of Jesus. So we can see how he deals with the situation.

First, he is strictly non-judgmental. All the people in this incident know that sin is present. What they need to know is its extent.

Secondly, he is very loving and gentle, to the rulers and the woman. In a situation of life and death, he is life.

Thirdly, he asks the right question, so that they can see the true issue.

Fourthly, in sending her on her way, there is no possibility of condoning what she has done, but there is every possibility for a new life for her.

So Jesus sees the real nature of the situation and therein his saving power is at work.

3. The disciples – who is the greatest?[9]

It is not necessary to look at each time Jesus deals with the disciples; but this particular incident is important. Again, notice the context. Some of them had just experienced the wonder of the Transfiguration, the others the frustration of not being able to heal the epileptic boy. Jesus had given another of his predictions of his passion and the disciples were, not surprisingly, insecure.

So an argument as to who is "the greatest" breaks out amongst them. Jesus waits for the right moment before asking what appears to be a completely innocuous question. Their silence indicates that, as it is exposed, the discussion is childish and futile. Jesus takes it seriously however. Childish and futile it may be, but it represents their real thoughts. He does not say that they must not think these thoughts – how can they not? It is part of their insecurity.

What Jesus does do, though, is to help them to see the true nature of greatness and the attitudes which produce greatness. So, servanthood and acceptance of the small and insignificant are the marks of the one who wants to be great. He gives them a yardstick far more stretching than worldly glory. That is all relative anyway and quickly forgotten. Acceptance of the apparently insignificant in life and of an attitude of mind which sees responsibility in terms of service leads to Jesus, and beyond to the Father. Again, look at what Jesus is showing us:

First, he takes the insecurity seriously, no matter in how trivial a manner it is expressed.

Secondly, he points them to the true issues – true greatness and true security.

He does not condemn them, nor does he tell them that they

are being silly. He is far too loving for that. In the putting of
the child in the midst, he uses a visual aid which focuses the
issues indelibly.

4.   Mary Magdalene[10]

Much has been written on Mary Magdalene, and Frank Lake
in particular has a great deal to say about her as a typical
hysteric.[11] I cannot assume, with him and others, that Mary
Magdalene is the same person as Mary the sister of Martha
and Lazarus. Nor can one assume that Mary is the prostitute
mentioned by Luke, Mark and Matthew, as having anointed
Jesus.[12] The only solid evidence we have, is that Mary was a
witness of the crucifixion[13] and of the resurrection, and this
is best seen in John's Gospel.[14]

Whatever one wants to make of her (and she does seem to
have many of the characteristics of a hysterical personality),
she was at the grave of Jesus, weeping uncontrollably. She
undoubtedly had reason. Surely, having come face to face
with Jesus, she knew life for the first time and a man who
cared when others appeared not to. Even that is conjecture.
But, weep she does – for a lost direction and a lost body, the
ultimate indignity. Jesus's appearance produces a rush of
words, a desperate hope that she may at least lay out the
corpse with dignity. More likely a physical point on which to
pin her hopes and lost aspirations. Even when she recognises
Jesus, he will not let her dependence upon him express itself
in touch. She is given something to do, which takes her out of
herself and gives her a sense of value in her own right, as a
witness to the resurrection. The focus here is quite specific –
and it works, for I have seen it happen.
First, the dependence is allowed to be expressed – though not
specifically encouraged.
Secondly, Jesus does not allow the dependence to continue.
There is a very clear injunction: "Do not touch me." The
point is that touching will not help. What does help is something which fulfils other more important needs in her.

Thirdly, those needs are to look outside herself and be useful. One can see Mary as one who might cling easily, but given something to do for someone she will do it with skill and tenacity. Given the correct insights, the Mary Magdalenes of this world are the evangelists waiting to be used – waiting to do whatever needs to be done. The element of simply sitting and enjoying God is there too. As long as it is God that she clings to, she will have a remarkable ministry.

5. Simon the Pharisee[15]

Perhaps my favourite incident in the life of Jesus involves Simon the Pharisee. This may well be because Simon is so like me – not *quite* a snob, but one who, when the chips are down, is likely to side with the snobs. In many ways, he is not typical of the Pharisees – perhaps the really harsh ones were in Jerusalem and, being out "in the district", Simon was inclined to be a little more accepting. Whatever his motivation for inviting Jesus to a meal, Simon draws the line at Jesus allowing himself to be the object of love and, it would appear, slobbering love at that. Jesus knows his thoughts. On this occasion, it probably would not take much insight on the part of Jesus to discern them. One look at Simon's face would be enough. The distaste, disgust would have to have shown through, for Simon's background more or less guaranteed that type of disapproval.

Jesus's response to Simon is important. He does not say "it's sinful to think like that", or "who are you to judge this woman?" He just tells a story, which, by its very simplicity, arrests the attention and demands a response from Simon. When Simon has judged correctly (it would have been a very stupid person who did not judge correctly), Jesus spells out the differences between the loving attitude of the woman and the starchy disapproval of Simon. Even then, Jesus does not put his explanation on a legal basis, but in relation to repentance and love. Essentially, the person who has little of which he is able to repent is able to love little, for there is so little

there which is truly lovable. The reverse is also true. So Simon
is caught in the Jesus trap. If he is able to accept it, there is
every chance of his coming to a new awareness of salvation
and life. So, let me sum up.

First, Jesus lets the woman express her love in her way.

Secondly, he allows Simon to express his disapproval in his
way.

Thirdly, he does not condemn, he simply draws the sort of
comparison which allows for growth – and judgment. But the
judgment, when it comes, is both gentle and firm. It leaves no
woolly alternatives; but it does not consign Simon to hell
either. He makes clear the issues which call for repentance
and love.

6.   The rich young man and Judas[16]

It may seem strange to lump these two together, but they are
in a similar category: of people whom Jesus frees to make
their own decisions, even when it means danger in the latter
case, to himself. The point is that both are free to go the
wrong way, though they will have to take the consequences
for what they do. We have looked at the rich young man
earlier, but let us look at him again.

He asks a question, the answer of which he is well aware.
He has kept the law and yet it would appear that he is not
happy. Jesus's injunction to him, to sell all that he has and
give the proceeds away, is something he cannot do – he is too
wealthy to cope with denial as radical as that. So, far from
following him, he goes his own way sadly. Jesus makes it clear
what his course of action is to be, but he does not force him to
take that action. There is no coercion; no moral or spiritual
blackmail; only a straight choice and the freedom to make it.
That is Jesus's way and he is no less loving when the wrong
choice is made.

We see this also in the case of Judas. All four Gospels
mention him as having entered a plot to get rid of Jesus. John
alone records the events at the table, which send Judas

scurrying into the night. That is of course very significant for John – for Judas is an agent of the forces of darkness which are seeking to extinguish the light. So it is a logical progression, which has Judas in the garden pointing out Jesus to the arresting party. Interestingly, the kiss is not mentioned in John, but the giving of the sop at the Last Supper *is* mentioned, and there the initiative belongs to Jesus. Not only is the initiative in Jesus's hands, but the sop itself is a sign of unbearable love. So, the one who has been entered by Satan is the one whom Jesus seeks to reach by way of the loving action. Even as he gives it, Jesus realises the die is cast; Judas has already set things in motion, and cannot go back.

The words of Jesus are therefore significant for us: "What you are going to do, do quickly." There is no sense in which he tries to stop him. He simply recognises that Judas *is* going to do what he believes is right, and Jesus accepts him and allows him to do it. That is the ultimate love of Jesus. To see what Judas is doing, to accept him as he is, in spite of the threat posed by Judas, and to allow him the freedom to do it. That his action of betrayal takes place in secrecy and under the cover of night, only makes it the more awful, and the contrast between darkness and light that much more stark and frightening.

So again the freedom which Jesus gives is the freedom which can only come from one who loves so much, that he would rather die than force people into a relationship with God, which would inevitably be superficial and spurious.

What does all this mean for the counsellor?

I have taken models from the Gospels with the avowed intention of showing how Jesus dealt with people in a variety of ways. We could no doubt continue the exercise, but the point is made. Jesus always takes people beyond where they are. He refuses to play intellectual games with Nicodemus, and confronts him with insights which engage not only his intellect, but his whole being, and in the process, helps him to a new boldness in life. The woman taken in adultery is not condemned; nor is the rich ruler, nor Judas. They are given alternatives and those alternatives judge and save (or condemn, as the case may be).

He allows that the disciples are insecure – and gives them a new vision of security; he accepts the heartbroken state of Mary Magdalene and gives her a task which takes her outside herself. He allows Simon to disapprove, but he gives him a new set of criteria for judging people and actions in the future.

In all of these, the lesson for counselling can be summed up in one word: discernment. Jesus sees beyond the superficial and the outward; he is not bound by a style of relationship; he lets each one develop uniquely and deals with it as uniquely. The overwhelming love which he has for each one is impressive and awe-inspiring, for it is the love which frees in a way that is itself somewhat frightening. In each case, the end product is freedom – freedom to accept and be saved, or reject and live out the consequences of godlessness. For the counsellor there must surely be the same goal. We are not to force people, nor allow them the sort of dependence which means that they cannot think for themselves. We are to love them into seeing beyond the pettiness of the present, to the more fundamental truths which need to be grasped.

So, in Jesus's discernment, he makes it possible for people to grow – and be responsible. And responsibility means the ability to know oneself so well that we are able to respond to him and his demands. To be responsible means to be free to accept myself in the same way that Jesus accepts me and live a life which reflects my decision. Whatever that decision, Jesus's love is unbroken and unaltered. Jesus himself may be subjected to rejection, fear, acceptance and love, but it makes no difference to the love which he gives out – even to the loveless.

So, the counsellor's task is to pray for discernment and allow the counsellee the freedom to react in the way which is for him most responsible. There is no place for blackmail or coercion, only for making sure that the issues are very clear. And that leads us to the next chapter.

Chapter 11

Directive and Non-directive Counselling

I suppose the previous chapter and this one are basically two parts of the same subject. I tried in Chapter 10 to show that the essential elements in Jesus's dealings with people are his preparedness to hear them, to let them be themselves, and to ask the right questions.

It is certainly true in the counselling process that the person who comes for help has already some idea of the issues and knows that he has a problem. He also knows that his problem is often of his own making, as a result of sin, selfishness, inadequacy or a host of other things. It may also be the result of the sin and selfishness of others. Whatever the cause, there is a good chance that he cannot see himself entirely. He can often feel areas he cannot see without knowing their source. So to him and to others, his behaviour is illogical and frustrating. I have a great deal of hidden and unaccountable anger in me, which spills over at the most awkward and difficult times. I know that I am reacting illogically, but there is little I seem able to do about it at the time. I have identified the area of my life from which this comes. I now have to repent, accept forgiveness for myself, and forgive others for their part (justifiable or not) in creating the feelings with which I live. Much of this anger is related to feelings of being unloved. As I grow in acceptance, so the anger dissipates and I can learn new patterns of freedom and relationships.

Anyone who enters into a counselling relationship does so with a jumble of feelings, thoughts, fears and sins. The question is how to deal with them. There seem to be two different ways of dealing with the problem. In over-simplified terms, they may be expressed as *directive* and *non-directive* forms of counselling and in the literature they are set in opposition to each other. That is a pity, because it is unnecessary. Perhaps it would be good to look briefly at each of them and then come back to see what we can learn from Our Lord about them.

Non-directive counselling is essentially a reaction to a style of counselling which can only be described as "advice-giving". Advice-giving sets up an unhealthy dependency of counsellee on counsellor, putting the counsellor in a position of making the decisions without either having shared the feelings or lived the history of the other person. The difficulty then is that the counsellee does not feel responsible, so can more easily find an excuse when things go wrong. The type of counselling which says, "If I were you, I would . . ." is not helpful, and certainly not biblical. That does not mean that all advice is gratuitous and wrong. There are many occasions when the counsellor will have to give advice, but it will always be of the information-giving variety, which helps a person take the next step. Thus advice about the best job to get; where to look; a good lawyer or doctor or gynaecologist; what is required in specifically defined circumstances may be necessary. But the counsellor should not do it for the person, for that would lead to an irresponsible dependence.

So non-directive counselling seeks to take the person where he is, and helps him to utilise his own inner resources to his advantage and growth. It does not allow for value judgments ("that is sinful") but is concerned to help the person grow in his own self-awareness to new standards of behaviour and confidence. It focuses almost all the counselling on feelings.

Listening requires that we "hear" the feelings hidden behind the spoken words. Listening empathises with the counsellee, being more concerned to relate to the feelings, so that there can be true acceptance. Remarks such as "You must have really hurt when . . ." are the stock-in-trade of the non-directive counsellor. That sort of remark will lead to further disclosures as the person responds to the counsellor's acceptance of him.

Essentially, then, non-directive counselling aims at helping the client to explore areas of feelings of which he has been hitherto unaware, and which have enslaved him. He is then to be helped to discover the solutions to his problems for himself and to act on them, so that he can exercise greater responsibility and freedom in the handling of his own life.

My main criticism of non-directive counselling is that it seems to so focus a man and his own resources, that there is little place for God and his resources. In its concern to take the person seriously it does not take the person seriously enough. It seems hesitant to allow the person the resources available to a Christian – the whole panorama of the Christian faith and spirituality. In trying not to be judgmental, it can so easily land up with no judgment at all; in trying not to be directive, it can allow the person no other direction than the one which he himself wants to take. And so he is deprived of much of the life-giving Christian perspective and direction. That it is done for the best possible reason does not make it any less of a problem.

Directive counselling assumes a different perspective, but has as its motive exactly that of the non-directive: to help people trapped in the agony of their own sinful condition. It is not advice-giving. Its purpose is to listen carefully and discover the sin in the situation so that Christian resources may be brought to bear on it and the person may repent, turn again and enter more fully into salvation.

The most important contribution to literature on directive counselling in recent years is Jay Adams's *Competent to Counsel*. It has much to commend it. Adams reacts to the non-directive Rogerian styles of counselling which, as I have suggested, concentrate on the counsellee's ability to find his own solutions, and which have held sway for so long. He quite unashamedly declares, as I do, that Jesus Christ is at the centre of all counselling and that man cannot, and should not, be taken as an end and entity in himself. Man is fully human only as he is recognised as being "in Christ". Adams writes of "nouthetic confrontation"[1] (a style of directive counselling which takes its name from the Greek words meaning "admonish", "warn", or "teach") against which a great deal of unjustified criticism has been levelled.

Adams suggests three basic elements in nouthetic counselling:

1.   "Nouthetic confrontation always implies a problem and presupposes an obstacle which must be overcome; something is wrong in the life of the one who is confronted[2] . . . nouthetic confrontation arises out of a condition in the counsellee that God wants changed".[3]

2.   It "presupposes a counselling type of confrontation in which the object is to effect a characterological and behavioural change in the counsellee".[4] The counselling here is not concerned with long excursions into the counsellee's past, but rather is "largely committed to a discussion of the what".[5] So what has happened and what can happen is essential to the nouthetic confrontation.

     In other words, its focus is problem-solving and on working out what is wrong, so that the problem can be defined and dealt with.

3.   "The goal must be to meet obstacles head on and overcome them verbally, not in order to punish, but to help him."[6] "*Nouthesis* is motivated by love and deep concern, in which clients are counselled and corrected by verbal means for their good, ultimately, of course, that God may be glorified."[7]

Now all of this is in many ways perfectly acceptable. There is no reason to think that the word of God, mediated through a counsellor, does not confront – in fact, as we have seen throughout this book, it *must* confront, for there is no other way for growth or salvation.

The difficulty I have with Adams is that at its worst (and I have had to pick up one or two victims of the worst of this type of counselling) it is highly manipulative. The person is re-

duced to a sinful heap, the confrontation is so hurtful and
damaging that the final state may be worse than the first. The
danger is that the problem becomes more important than the
person, and problem-solving can so easily become a substitute for the love which frees and changes. Most people know
their sin; what they need to experience is the acceptance
which makes it possible for them to grow in self-esteem and
come to a new vision of love, which only God can give.

Also, directive counselling seems to me (especially as I read
Adams), to be short on listening. Its concern is to get to the
problem and, in the process, Adams pours unnecessary scorn
on anything which is non-directive. While I have many of the
same criticisms as he of the Rogerian approach, his nouthetic
confrontation can, it seems to me, be as harsh and rigid as the
Rogerian style appears flaccid and directionless. Both are
unbiblical. The fact that directive confrontation is at times a
very necessary help to certain types of problem, does not
mean that it is helpful and right in every circumstance.

Adams's unnecessary lampooning of different styles of
counselling[8] is itself a harsh rejection of much that is
important.[9] He need not ride his own system on the back of
others; it can stand in its own right.

My final and most strenuous objection to Adams is that, in
advocating a system, he does not, in fact, do justice to the
pattern which Jesus gives us. Yes, of course Jesus calls us to
repentance; of course he calls us to salvation and new life in
him; of course he calls us to faith, but he does not prescribe
how it is done, nor does he insist that it can only be done one
way. His criticism of the religious leaders of his day was not
that the Law was ineffective, but that those who applied the
Law did not in fact live by it – or in the spirit of it. Adams is so
busy tilting at the Rogerian windmills, that he does not
recognise that he has fallen into the prescriptive trap at the
opposite end of the field.

Let us now look again at Jesus's style. (I make no apology for
this section being little more than a reminder of much we have

already discussed.) We will start with Martha and Mary.[10]
The fascinated Mary is so glued to Jesus's words that she is
unable to hear the increasing crash of the pots and pans as
Martha's irritation gets the better of her. Finally, unable to
bear it, full of the housewife's woes when there is too much to
do and not enough help, Martha complains to Jesus. Jesus's
response to her is not, as presumably the nouthetic counsellor's would be: "Mary go and help Martha; that will solve her
problem, and you can come and listen later." Nor does he
recognise her anger and empathise with it, which would be the
non-directive approach: (You feel hurt that Mary is not
taking you seriously.) No – he gives Martha another way of
looking at things. (Notice, incidentally, that there is no
either/or between Martha and Mary. So often one hears a
person, usually a woman, justify her activism by saying
something like "of course I am a Martha, not a Mary". But
that is not justified from the text. At best, it is wishful
thinking!) So Martha is not told to sit down and join Mary,
nor the other way around. Martha is told that her anxiety is
causing her to become bothered about all sorts of things, none
of which are important. To sit with Mary at the feet of Jesus
may mean the supper is late, or they might eat differently,
possibly more simply, but all will be better off. In some ways,
it reflects Jesus's saying in Matthew, "seek first his kingdom
and his righteousness, and all these things shall be yours as
well".[11] So, he neither prescribes a solution, nor does he
simply listen intently. He gives her a new dimension of
self-awareness, which is liberating because of the love which
changes her perspectives.

Jesus's relationship with his disciples is revealing in this
regard. He calls them[12] and expects a response. But "follow
me" is more than "come with me" – it is a new way of living.
They abandon their old way of life, be it fishing or tax
collecting, and come on a totally uncharted course. That is
always Jesus's way; the choice is direct – the way is his alone.
Later, when Peter comes looking for him as he prays at a
lonely place,[13] he refuses to go back to the clamour of people

looking for him. Instead, he moves onwards to unbroken ground.

As he sends the twelve out, with authority to preach and cast out demons,[14] the pattern is the same. There are no neat answers, no formulae, only the wonder of people going out in the power of Jesus. No blueprint, only the loving authority of the one who meets sin in every form. So we could go on. But, there are other elements too. The later sending of the Twelve[15] is even less prescriptive. It reflects for them only an attitude and a simplicity of purpose which is all they need to meet the demands of their mission. Later still, when children were being brought to him,[16] he changes the perspectives of the disciples, not by reprimanding them, but by refusing to allow himself to be put into the box of "too busy" or "too tired". By not allowing that box to exist, he shows the disciples the true nature of discipleship and life. Receiving the childlike seeing that type of person for what he is, means a new direction, a new way of living. When James and John want the place of glory,[17] he does not tell them that their attitude is sinful and they must snap out of it if they want to be saved. He hears their insecurities, accepts their feelings and then gives them a style of living which is totally outside their comprehension, but which will meet their needs.

So then we can see that Jesus is neither non-directive, nor directive in the way that the schools of counselling would advocate. He does direct, in a way which is his alone. But he also points people within themselves, to see the true nature of things and comprehend new attitudes. He will not be boxed, or put into categories; he breaks out of them with a new way of living and a new way of dying. Life in Christ means going confidently into each situation, armed only with his authority and motivated only by that which gives glory to God. That is the aim of all counselling, not that we should follow a "school", or style of counselling, but that we should be the agents whereby people are helped to live confidently in Jesus.

Confidence means being prepared to take risks. One of my most precious memories was an occasion when a person whom I had been counselling took a risk with glorious results. He had lived his life as a failure. Everything he had done had never quite worked. He was dominated by mother and mocked at school. Without self-confidence and with hardly any self-acceptance, he arrived at the college by a route of much rejection. Someone had eventually seen past the exterior to the person waiting to emerge and he was accepted for training. His initial time at the college was inevitably not easy. In several hours of counselling he came to see that he could go no further, unless he took a risk and faced the possibility of rejection – again. So one college meeting he stood up and gave us all blazes for keeping the common room in a mess. The look on his face when the whole body spontaneously applauded is forever etched on my memory. They recognised the risk and responded, not with rejection, but love. It not only made his day, it made it possible for him to start living confidently. In the process of counselling, I had said to him, "Unless you are prepared to take a risk, you will stay where you are and never grow." It was not for me to say more – anything else would have taken from him the responsibility of acting on his own.

Risky living is at the heart of commitment. The extent to which a person is prepared to take risks in relationships and life is the extent to which we must be prepared to direct or not in counselling. If we look, for example, at one or two other incidents relating to Jesus, we may well see it more clearly. In so many instances Jesus helps people – and sometimes forces people – to look at the right issues, ask the right questions, and face the right problems. But he also at times refuses to deal with the issues directly. When the person in the multitude requests that Jesus should take his side against that of his brother in the question of their inheritance,[18] Jesus does not even deal with the question. He simply mentions that he is not a "judge or divider" and then goes on to warn them against the problems of covetousness, following it with the parable about the man who built larger barns to prepare for a future which never materialised. Those of us who have had anything to do with deceased estates will know why Jesus spoke thus. In this case, he points the covetous brother to a totally different way of living, where greed is not a necessity.

Again, the attitudes of the people are at the heart of new life in him. So he must perforce point out hypocrisy where he sees it. The woman bent over for eighteen years[19] is clearly less important than an ox or a donkey in the eyes of those who are responsible for the maintenance of the Law in Judaism. Jesus makes them recognise the double standards inherent in their attitudes. Counselling must do that, whether it is by helping the person to the courage of self-evaluation, or by confrontation will depend very largely on the attitude of the counsellee. There have been times when I have had to use the confrontational approach; more often one must use something no less effective but very much more gentle.

I think of an occasion when I used a very heavy confrontational attitude with a person who simply could not handle it. His whole life had been one of rejection and scorn from his father. All he could hear from me was his father rejecting him again. It took me a long time to get past the pain of that first interview and help him to a measure of self-acceptance which allowed him to see the hypocrisy of his double dealing for himself. That he was sinful was not the question. How he was helped to see it was the important thing.

So we could go on. The purpose of counselling is to help the person to come face to face with the saving, healing love of Christ. Nothing else matters. For the counsellor to worry what technique he is committed to is for him to forget his aim and to forget the counsellee. His only aim is the health and well being of the person counselled.

So, finally, let me sum up. Forget the school of counselling you belong to; forget your pride; forget yourself and focus on Jesus. He alone makes the difference, and he alone is the Saviour – of the counsellor and counsellee. In him is hope, the confident expectation of new life, lived for others and to his glory. There is no power outside the power of God, to which we can turn. We may have the finest counselling techniques, but if we have not the Spirit of Christ, we will lack the discernment, the love and the vision to see past ourselves, and past the obvious, to the areas of failure, sin, inadequacy and self-rejection, which are the cause of so many problems. It is the extent to which we as counsellors can counsel with at least some of the counselling of Jesus that we will fulfil that part of the counselling ministry to which we have been called.

Chapter
12

Man and Sin

The view of man and sin which Jesus inherited is surprisingly complicated yet has a delightful directness and simplicity. It starts with a vision of perfection, of God's explosive yet purposeful creativity which culminates in man, who is to exercise authority while remaining under authority.

The Bible does not bother to reflect on the question, "What is man?" That is irrelevant. Man is a creature made in the image of God. The Hebrew word for "image" implies the imprint left in wax by a seal or signet ring. It is authoritative and definitive, reflecting the presence of the one whose seal it is. It is the creatureliness of man which is constantly emphasised. He is God's representative, but he is not God. To say that he is is the essence of sin. In the perfection of God's creation the dependence of man on God, and the dependence of the rest of creation under man is the way God would have it. So the need for man to be obedient and under authority is a powerful theme in the first two chapters of Genesis.

In Genesis 1:27 we have the repetition of "bara" – "create" – three times. The same word is used in v. 1 to signify the whole process; now it is used repeatedly in one sentence to emphasise that we have reached the very pinnacle of creation, man. Man as he reflects God's attributes; man in the glory of his sexuality; man blessed and powerful as he lives under authority and exercises the authority of God.

There is no more sublime insight into man, except perhaps as it is extended and developed in Genesis 2. By the end of Chapter 1, we see him in all his perfection, showing the presence of God in his life, through obedience; in his sexuality; in his ability to exercise authority within creation. We see him at one with God and creation – he is indeed glorious. This picture is extended in Genesis 2:4b–24. Here the emphasis is the same, even if the way of telling is somewhat different. From man to order. Here man (adam) is made from dust or clay (adamah), moulded and formed, as God the creator fashions him to the shape and stature that he wants. God breathes his breath (ruah) into him and man lives; dependent on a God who creates so that man may have dominion over all the plants in Eden.[1] The same sense of dominion is reflected in Chapter 1. Man is given authority over the plants, with the exception of the tree of life. The authority is extended further. Man becomes the "naming animal". As God creates the various animals, so man names them, and those names stand. In the Old Testament, to know the name and to pronounce it implies authority and power over the one named. Here man is given authority to choose the name and thus to "Have dominion" over the animals. The motive for creation is specifically for the purpose of community. Man is not to live in isolation, but within the community of marriage and family.

The gift of the woman is therefore the high point of Genesis 2. Here the male (ish) responds with enthusiastic joy to the female (ishshah). There is no shame, only an acceptance of sexuality as part of God's creativity and the recognition that nakedness does not lead to shame. It is after the fall that nakedness becomes something to cover and fear.

Man is therefore a responsible, authoritative and community-centred creature, whose life is to be lived in obedience to God and joyfully at work in creation. There is a disarming little sentence in Genesis 2: "The Lord God took the man and put him in the garden of Eden to till it and keep it."[2] So life with God is not an eternity of perpetual laziness and sensual delights; no dancing girls, sheep's eyes and sherbet, and endless days of doing nothing and being less; it is lived to God's glory and in joyful obedience to Him.

Sin

If the vision of perfection described in Chapters 1 and 2 of Genesis give us a picture of a loving God who desires unity and harmony in creation, then the key to man's condition today is in the lie spoken by the serpent to the woman in Chapter 3. "You will not die"[3] is man's illusion, and try as he may, he cannot escape death. In fact he goes each day closer to a global death and tragically he goes happily and unthinkingly, as he abandons God, and seeks to do things his way.

I am aware of the illusions. As I sit here writing I am aware that the hell of racism is all around me, that men are at war all over the world, that most of the world is hungry tonight, that those who have the money in this land are worried that those who do not have it will steal it from them; that murder, greed, rape, violence, drunkenness and all the rest will erupt tonight. I know that those who have power will be holding on to it, and those who do not will be plotting or dreaming in some way or another to acquire it. I know that today the arms build-up is so great that, humanly speaking, nothing can stop us destroying each other. I know that tonight adultery will be performed, fornication undertaken under the pretext of adult behaviour, marriages will break, suicide will be committed, wives will be swopped, children will be beaten, prisoners tortured and men and women will die of despair, loneliness, fear and isolation; and most people will not care at all. I know that tonight the earth is one step closer to choking to death as greedy, avaricious man overexploits its natural resources and pollutes what we have for the sake of higher profit margins, or the myth of "progress". Because of one fateful promise – "You will not die" – the world which God loves so much is happily and swiftly embarked upon a living death.

The tragedy of man is that he abandons the wonder of unity with God for a real belief that he can somehow "go it alone"; that he is the master of his own fate, that he is better off without God; that he can exploit creation to his own advantage and to satisfy his own greed, and that in the process he "will not die". The biblical picture is uncompromising. It says something like this: "If you think that you 'will not die', you will take the consequences and those consequences will lead to the living death you believe you will avoid."

As in the first two chapters of Genesis, the question is not "What is sin?" – it is a clear picture – "if you want to know what has happened to the world, then look here and you will see". Sin is not to be discussed and wondered at, it is to be recognised for what it is, without compromise, or even condonation. It is not a minor disruption but a major, traumatic event which affects every aspect of life and perverts everything to which man puts his hand. Genesis 3 and 4:1–16 show a progression of rejection of God, which leads to the living death of which we have been speaking.

It starts with the very simple process of doubting God's word. Notice here that the serpent is not Satan, or even a demonic creature. He is no more than the cleverest of all other wild animals, "more subtle", as the RSV has it.[4] This means that he is one who can think more clearly, even more deviously, but he is not Satan. Sin, at this point, does not need Satan, it needs man's rebellion. And man *wants* to rebel, he is only looking for an excuse to do so.

Rebellion does not just happen; sin is very attractive. It offers power and independence for the best possible reasons. So the process of rationalisation is the next step in the worry process.[5] Essentially the excuses are very clever and very effective. They involve the need to eat, the need for beauty and the need for wisdom. All in the right place are essential, but when abused they offer so much more, which they can never produce. Each of them is an end in itself when looked at as an excuse. For sin the end is not the expected life, but death.

So the woman took the fruit, ate it, gave it to the man, he ate it. No crashing thunder, no terrifying flash of lightning, no earthquake, wind or voice from Heaven. They are simply suddenly aware that they are naked and ashamed. With shame comes the need to cover themselves. Then because they feel shame, they are afraid, so they hide. Naked and ashamed they are confronted by God and there they move into the next step of the process – buckpassing. The man blames the woman and, by implication, God: "The woman whom *thou* gavest to be with me – *she* gave me fruit."[6] The woman blames the serpent and all come under the judgment of God. Dismissed from Eden they face the harshness of a creation now strangely unproductive.

The story is not complete, however. Cain and Abel[7] escalate sin, as jealousy and then murder find their way into history. Murder gives way to a more complicated attempt to cover up, and that in turn to the terrible statement of indifference: "Am I my brother's keeper?"[8] The worst is still to come, for Cain, unable now to trust himself, cannot trust man or God,[9] and even when God gives him a mark of protection, he can no longer live at ease.

So perhaps that is where we should leave things. Man created in a vision of joyful obedience is shattered by shame, fear, anger, indifference and a joyless lack of trust.

Jesus is our Saviour; he experienced it all and gave us a new way of living. Let us pray that as counsellors we are ourselves so aware of the power and presence of Jesus in our lives that we may lead others through the fears and shame to new life in obedience to him.

Notes

Introduction

1 Seward Hiltner, *Pastoral Counselling*, Abingdon Press 1949.
2 Howard J. Clinebell Jr, *Basic Types of Pastoral Counselling*, Abingdon Press 1966.
3 Carrol A. Wise, *Pastoral Counselling, Its Theory and Practice*, Harper 1951.
4 Rollo May, *The Art of Counselling*, Abingdon Press 1939.
5 Frank Lake, *Clinical Theology*, Darton, Longman & Todd 1966. This is Lake's magnum opus, though in many ways it is too detailed and as such is not as helpful as it might be.
6 Jay E. Adams, *Competent to Counsel*, Presbyterian Reformed Publishing Co. 1970, p. 91.
7 It is probably true that nouthetic counselling as advocated by Adams is almost entirely directive – though he might disclaim this. Certainly the Rogerian reaction against "advice-giving" has led to a non-directive counselling, which *on its own* does not seem to me to be terribly helpful in the long term. Hiltner's definition, "to help people to help themselves", is only part of the over-all process of counselling.
8 Ruth Carter Stapleton, *The Gift of Inner Healing*, Hodder & Stoughton 1977.
9 Kenneth McAll, *Healing the Family Tree*, Sheldon 1982.
10 Frank Lake, *Tight Corners in Pastoral Counselling*, Darton, Longman & Todd 1981.
11 Roger F. Hurding, *Restoring the Image*, Paternoster 1980.

Chapter 1 – Abba

1 Mk 1:15; Mt. 4:17.
2 Cf. Mt. 7:28; Mk 1:22; 1:27 for a few examples.

3   J. Jeremias, *New Testament Theology*, SCM 1971, p. 67.
4   Ibid., p. 65.
5   Lk. 23:46.
6   Jeremias, op. cit., p. 59
7   Ibid., p. 61.
8   Cf. Is. 49:4; 50:7; 52:13–53:12.
9   Mark's insistence on Jesus's use of his exousia in his ministry is always related to an absolute demand for obedience on those who come under his authority. This, in turn, implies an absolute obedience to that same authority. Without it, he would not be able to exercise authority.
10   Mk 14:36.
11   Lk. 2:49.
12   Lk. 2:51.
13   Lk. 2:52.
14   Lk. 4:1.
15   Mk 14:32–6; Mt. 26:36–9; Lk. 22:39–46.
16   Lk. 4:16–30.
17   Mk 3:4.
18   Mk 2:25.
19   Mt. 8:19–20.
20   Mk 14:50.
21   Mk 14:66–72.
22   Mk 15:21–37.
23   Mk 10:35–40.
24   Mk 11:15–17; Mt. 21:12, 13; Lk. 19:45–6; Jn 2:13–16.
25   Mk 8:33.
26   Lk. 13:31–3.
27   Jn 10:30.
28   Rom. 8:12–17.
29   Adams, op. cit., pp. xi–xxii.

Chapter 2 – Listening

1   Adams, op. cit., pp. 87ff.
2   Mk 10:35–46.
3   Mk 10:49.
4   Ibid.
5   Mk 5:1–20.
6   Mk 5:22.

7 Mk 5:30.
8 Mk 8:17.
9 Jn 6:60.
10 Jn 6:66–9.
11 Jn 4:1–42.
12 Jn 4:6.
13 Jn 4:39.
14 Jn 3:1–21.
15 Jn 3:2.
16 Jn 3:21.
17 Jn 7:50–1.
18 Mt. 12:9–12.
19 Mt. 15:1–9.
20 Mk 12:13–17.
21 Mk 8:15; Lk. 12:1.
22 Mt. 8:5–12.
23 Mk 7:25–30.
24 Mt. 16:13–20.
25 Lk. 19:41–4.
26 Jn 11:32–6.
27 Mk 6:34.
28 Mk 1:40–1.
29 Mk 6:5–6.
30 Lk. 6:12.
31 Adams, op. cit., pp. 78–104.

Chapter 3 – Fear

1 Mt. 10:28.
2 Jer. 1:5.
3 Gal. 1:15.
4 For a full discussion of this, see Lake, *Tight Corners in Pastoral Counselling*, Ch. 2.
5 Virginia Axline, *Dibs in Search of Self*, Penguin 1971.
6 Ibid., pp. 76ff.
7 Ibid., pp. 69–70.
8 Gen. 1:2.
9 Exod. 15:8.
10 Gen. 7:17–24.
11 Thus in Ps. 32:6 the Psalmist is aware of "a time of great distress, in the rush of great waters".

12 Ps. 69:1–2.
13 Ps. 69:4.
14 Rev. 21:1.
15 Gen. 2:5.
16 Gen. 3:19.
17 Ps. 22:15.
18 Cf also Ps. 22:29: "The proud of the earth shall bow down; before him shall bow all who go to the dust; and he who cannot keep himself alive."
19 Ps. 78:19.
20 Cf. Mk 1:12–13.
21 Mt. 12:43.
22 Mk 1:12–13.
23 Just looking at Mark's Gospel and taking only one example each, we see him with (1) demons 1:23–6; (2) sickness 1:30–1; paralysis 2:1–12; leprosy 1:40–4; (3) hardness of heart 3:1–6; (4) chaos: wind and water 4:35–41; desert 8:1–10; (5) fear of death 14:32–40; (6) death in others 5:35–42 (though the most obvious example there would be the raising of Lazarus in Jn 11); in his own death and the darkness of chaos present at the same time 15:33–9.
24 Mk 5:15.
25 Mk 1:24–7.
26 Mk 4:35–41.
27 Mk 4:40 – the disciples are told they are "cowards" or "fearful".
28 Mk 5:36.
29 Mk 6:45–52.
30 Jn 11:1–44.
31 Jn 1:5.
32 Mk 4:41.
33 N. Tate and N. Brady (1696) in the hymn, the first line of which runs: "Through all the changing scenes of life."
34 Carter Stapleton, op. cit.
35 1 Jn 4:18.

Chapter 4 – Anxiety

1 Victor Frankl, *Man's Search for Meaning*, Washington Square Press 1969. Frankl insists that logotherapy tries to help the

person to see himself in relation to the future rather than the past, thereby facing the future by changing his attitudes. Logotherapy thus uses the experiences of the past and present, especially those of love and suffering, to bring about a positive and loving response to the future. That is as I understand it. Frankl discusses it at length on pp. 151–214.

2 Mt. 6:25–34.
3 Mt. 6:24.
4 Lk. 12:1–34.
5 Lk. 12:8–12.
6 Lk. 12:13–21.

Chapter 5 – Anger

1 Mt. 5–7.
2 Mt. 5:3–9, 10–12.
3 Mt. 5:38–48.
4 Mt. 5:21–6.
5 Jn 7:14–24.
6 Jn 7:15.
7 The parables are so realistic that we tend to think of them as historical events. They are not – they are traps to catch us and bring us into the Kingdom of God. They force us to take seriously what we are and why we are what we are; they require a decision from us as to our priorities and commitments. They are *not* useful illustrations for preaching or Sunday school lessons. That they are too often used thus says something about our preaching and educational programmes.
8 Lk. 15:11–32.
9 Mk 3:6 and Mk 14:1, 2, 10, 11.
10 Mk 14:53–65.
11 Mk 14:62 and Lk. 22:71.
12 Mk 15:1–15; Mt. 27:11–26; Lk. 23:18–27.
13 Lk. 23:34.
14 Jn 19:26–7.
15 Lk. 23:39–43.
16 Mk 15:34.
17 Lk. 23:46.
18 Jn 19:30.
19 Rom. 12:21.

Chapter 6 – Self-acceptance

1   Hurding, op. cit., p. 14.
2   Jn 12:43.
3   Mk 8:36; cf. Mk 8:34–8
4   Mk 8:29.
5   Mt. 11:28–30.
6   Mk 12:31; Mt. 22:39; Lk. 10:27.
7   Lev. 19:18.
8   Lk. 6:31–6.
9   *Martyrdom of Polycarp*, IX, 3.
10 Acts 7:60.
11 Lk. 12:24.
12 Lk. 12:28.
13 Lk. 15:1–10.
14 Mt. 15:24.
15 Mk 2:15–17.
16 Lk. 18:10–14.
17 Lk. 19:1–10.
18 Mt. 21:28–32.
19 Mk 2:13–14.
20 Mk 2:15–17.
21 Phil. 3:17.
22 1 Cor. 4:16; 11:1.
23 Cf. 2 Cor. 1:12; 2 Cor. 4:6ff; 2 Cor. 5:14; 1 Cor. 9:19ff.
24 Cf. 2 Cor. 11:21–12:10 and Phil. 3:2–16.

Chapter 7 – Repentance and forgiveness

1   Mk 10:46–52.
2   Adams, op. cit.
3   Mk 1:4; Lk. 3:3.
4   Mk 1:15.
5   Lk. 15:7, 10.
6   Lk. 15:11–32.
7   Lk. 15:17.
8   Lk. 19:8.
9   Mt. 6:2, 5, 16.
10 Mt. 6:7.
11 Jeremias, op. cit., pp. 155ff.
12 Mt. 18:3.

13 Jeremias, op. cit., p. 156.
14 Mk 10:17.
15 Mt. 6:14–15.
16 Mt. 18:21–2.
17 Lk. 17:1–4.
18 Lk. 17:5.
19 Mt. 18:23–35.
20 Mk 2:10; Mt. 9:6; Lk. 5:24.
21 Lk. 7:36–50.
22 Acts 7:60.
23 Eph. 1:7, 8.
24 Col. 1:13–14.
25 Acts 2:14–36.
26 Acts 2:37–8.
27 I do not normally believe that "tongues" is the only guarantee of the presence of the Spirit of God, but in this *particular* situation I believe it is essential that the person is thus filled and expresses it accordingly. "Tongues" is a gift from God which can be therapeutic in helping the person to accept the living Spirit into the void left by the departed demon. If tongues does not ensue the counsellor has no way of knowing whether the Spirit has entered into the person in a situation which is inevitably highly tension-filled and emotional.

Chapter 8 – Giving and receiving

1 Gen. 2:18.
2 Guy Butler, *Karoo Morning* and *Bursting World*, David Philip, 1979 and 1983.
3 Eph. 5:21.
4 Hurding, op. cit., p. 113.
5 Acts 20:35.
6 Mk 10:45.
7 Jn 13:1–20.
8 Jn 13:20.
9 Mk 4:24–5.
10 Lk. 20:9–16.
11 Lk. 19:11–27.
12 Lk. 19:11–27.
13 Mt. 25:31–46.

14   Mk 9:33–7.
15   William Temple, *Readings in St John's Gospel*, Macmillan 1959, p. 210.
16   Mk 6:10–11.
17   Jn 1:11–12.
18   Jn 14:16–17.
19   Lk. 17:11–19.
20   Lk. 7:36–50.
21   Mt. 26:26–9 (Matthew has the fullest version of this incident outside the passage at 1 Cor. 11:23–6).
22   Mt. 11:19.
23   Lk. 19:1–10
24   Lk. 10:38–42 and Jn 11.
25   Mk 1:41 – the Greek word *splangthnistheis* is translated "moved with pity" in the RSV, but the noun *splangthnon* is the word for the bowels – and hence the seat of the emotions.
26   Jn 3:28–30.

Chapter 9 – The love of God in counselling

1   Jn 1:12.
2   Jn 3:16.
3   Langenhoven's *The Shadow of Nazareth* (that is an English translation of the title of a book I have only come across in Afrikaans) is long since out of print. It made a deep impression on me when I was introduced to it more than thirty years ago. I have always believed that it ought to have been republished – though I wonder if that is not simply a youthful memory which would not stand up today.
4   Deut. 6:5.
5   Lev. 19:1–35.
6   Lev. 19:18.
7   G. von Rad, *Deuteronomy*, SCM Press 1966, p. 63.
8   Ernest Gordon, *Miracle on the River Kwai*, Fontana 1963.
9   Lk. 15:20–4.
10   Lk. 20:9–18.
11   Lk. 19:12–27.
12   Cf Mt. 22:1–14 and the memorable parables in Ch. 25.
13   Jn 2:13–22.
14   Jn 3:16.

15   Jn 3:19.
16   Jn 15, 16, 17.
17   Jn 15:23, 24.
18   Jn 17:15–18.
19   Mt. 1:18–25.
20   Mt. 2:13–18.
21   1 Jn 4:18.
22   Gal. 6:14.
23   Rom. 5:8.
24   Mk 8:27ff.
25   Mk 8:31ff; 9:30ff; 10:33ff.
26   Mk 8:31.
27   Mk 9:31.
28   Mk 10:33.
29   Clinebell, op. cit., pp. 222–43.

Chapter 10 – Models

1   Clinebell, op. cit.
2   Ibid., pp. 46–9.
3   Jn 3:1–21.
4   Jn 3:3.
5   Jn 3:7–15.
6   Jn 7:45–52.
7   Jn 19:39.
8   Jn 7:58–8:11.
9   Mk 9:33–7.
10   Jn 20:1–18.
11   Lake, *Clinical Theology*, pp. 446–59.
12   Lk. 7:36–8; Mk 14:3–9; Mt. 26:6–13. Only Luke mentions that the woman was "of the city, who was a sinner".
13   Mk 15:40–7; Mt. 27:56.
14   Jn 20:1–18.
15   Lk. 7:36–50.
16   Lk. 18:18–23; Jn 13:21–30 and 18:1–4.

Chapter 11 – Directive and non-directive counselling

1   Adams, op. cit., p. 44 and *passim.*

2   Ibid., p. 44.
3   Ibid., p. 45.
4   Ibid., p. 46.
5   Ibid., p. 48.
6   Ibid., p. 50.
7   Ibid., p. 50.
8   Ibid. pp. 103–4.
9   Ibid., p. 103.
10 Lk. 10:38–42.
11 Mt. 6:33.
12 Mk 1:16–20; 2:13–14.
13 Mk 1:35–8.
14 Mk 3:13–15.
15 Mk 6:7–13.
16 Mk 10:13–16.
17 Mk 10:35ff.
18 Lk. 12:13–21.
19 Lk. 13:10–17.

Chapter 12 – Man and sin

1   Gen. 2:15.
2   Gen. 2:15.
3   Gen. 3:4.
4   Gen. 3:1.
5   Gen. 3:6.
6   Gen. 3:12.
7   Gen. 4:1–16.
8   Gen. 4:9.
9   Gen. 4:14.